WANDERLUST

Published in Sydney, Australia, by Zulu Alpha Press a registered
trademark. www.zulualphapress.com

In some instances, names, dates, location, and other details have been
changed to protect the identity and privacy of those discussed in this
book.

Cover design by David Provolo

Printed and bound in Australia.

ISBN 978-0-6484692-0-9

WANDERLUST

HOW I LEARNED TO RETHINK LOVE AND UNLEARN LUST

STEPHEN PETER ANDERSON

For Dad.

Our tendency to wander is matched by God's willingness to pursue.

— ANONYMOUS

CONTENTS

INTRODUCTION

On a shelf above my computer sits a faux wooden frame I bought from a dollar store. A dishevelled page with an uneven fold sits inside. The top half displays a short typed paragraph—a personal email I once received from Christian author Philip Yancey. I say personal because it's his own words—typed by him, not some automated copy-and-paste response with a digital signature alluding to its authenticity. His reply was to an email I had written him years ago, thanking him for his books while also giving context as to how his words helped shape my own life. His books spoke to me in a heartfelt way at a time when I was disillu-sioned about a lot of things, especially God. For some reason, his outlook on faith made up for the boredom I often felt while sitting in a church pew every Sunday. I also wanted to encourage him (not that he needed mine), and I received an unexpected encouragement in return. Naturally, I was surprised to hear anything from him at all, especially on Christmas Eve; it was a gift that trumped those under the tree waiting to be opened the next day. The reason I still keep the email isn't because it's a memento or some fan-obsessed shrine, but because it serves as a constant reminder, especially the last paragraph. In it he thanks me for the important reminder, 'The effort to be faithful in writing is worth it.' Then he signs off with a prompt to spur me on: 'Now, pick up your torch and show me.' In some weird way I've always felt compelled to pick up my proverbial torch (the illuminated hue of a MacBook) and honour that. Writing has always been something I've loved. From a young age I have longed to tell a story, but, like many, I was either too daunted by the task or I never felt I had one to tell. Sometimes you don't choose what to write, it chooses you. I felt a narrative tugging at me all along like a toddler vying for attention until it was heard. As I listened I realised I had a story and no choice but to tell it.

My friends call me Mysterio, not because I possess some sort of super mutant skills but because they believe I have one foot in the shadows. I'm not some secret operative; I'm just selective with whom I choose to reveal information. I don't share my political grievances on Facebook or spout a Twitter tirade over supermarket fails. Quite frankly, divulging information to the masses frightens me. But it doesn't mean I hold all my cards to my chest. I'm honest enough to share parts of my life when I feel comfortable enough or I need to. I tend to categorise my vulnerable moments and then dish them out to the people in my life I've carefully selected, like an army officer barking orders to those with different skill sets within his regiment. I've managed this way of life by compartmentalising my relationships, like an IKEA showroom. It was never a healthy approach, but it helped to give me a sense of structure and order. On the one hand, I mastered the ability to hide things. I would selectively divulge personal information between friends. Sometimes they would catch wind of things they weren't privy to and naturally take offence. Conducting confidential information often requires multitasking or a great personal assistant. Choosing to be selective isn't popular, but neither is over-sharing. A need-to-know basis is all anyone ever needs to know. And, on the other hand, while I assumed to possess some sort of control over my life, the reality was quite the opposite. My 'skill' of retaining privacy gnawed at me. Things I should've shared at a very early age I kept hidden, and hidden very well. Worst of all, I often manipulated moments of accountability, which made any acknowledgement extraneous. You cannot assume accountability if you're the one deciding what and with whom to be account-able to. It's all or nothing. There is no in-between. I say all of this to give you context of my controlled isolation—how for years I tried to steer the wheel of my beaten vessel down a very lonely road instead of stopping to ask for directions. My guarded privacy would eventually become as much of a comical irony as it was an obligation.

So here I find myself at the precipice of publishing a book that is anything but private. As any writer knows, part of the job naturally offers a biographical benefaction. If you want to share the truth, you have to be vulnerable enough to put yourself out there—no half measures. In my case, it feels like my final option in making sense of my thoughts and experiences. But before I put pen to paper, my honesty needed more than the approval of an editor, so I ran the idea for a story past my wife one night over dinner. I told her everything, explaining how it culminated in my desire to write a book. As I recall, it wasn't the easiest of revelations.

"So what name are you going to use?" she asked.

"Name? You mean the title of the book?" I answered.

"No, your name," she emphasised.

"What will it be?" I echoed.

I had no idea what she was asking or why she didn't seem too bothered with the subject.

"You know, a fictitious name." She snapped her fingers as if to keep up to the beat of a jazz melody. "What do they call it in the publishing world?"

I finally understood what she meant.

"Pseudonym!" I blurted.

"Yesss!" She clapped her hands together like two crashing cymbals.

"Why would I use that?" I quipped.

"Well, you know. . ." She exaggerated her eyebrow-raising like someone from a Monty Python skit.

"No, I don't," I interjected. I did. But I didn't feel it deserved any acknowledgement. A suggestive tennis match ensued.

"What would be the point?" I returned the serve.

"I don't know. It's just a very *different* book."

I refused to punish her with any more passive hints, so I said what she was thinking.

"So what you're saying is because this book is about sex will my name on the cover draw attention to all of us, including our extended family, potentially placing them in awkward conversations with people? Am I right?"

She returned with a soft-serve volley.

"Maybe."

Her maybe was a yes. My voice softened, and my eyes locked elsewhere but on her. I thought about what she said, and it was some moments before I felt I could respond judiciously.

"Believe me when I say that I've also thought about this, and as much as this book feels like it's an intimate account about me, it isn't Mötley Crüe's, *The Dirt*. There aren't any sordid confessions of unadulterated and debauched goings-on. It's about asking questions I myself struggled to answer for years. Can lust and love coexist? Do we live in a world where sexual conditioning governs our intimate behaviours? Why do we struggle with unwanted sexual desires? In asking myself these questions others might be open to think upon them no matter how awkward or uncomfortable."

I knew she understood what I meant. A part of her knew that this was as much a healing process as a vital proclamation that I felt needed to be heard. In my previous attempts to write this book, there was some internal resistance. It took daily reminding as to my sole purpose for wanting to write it. It all culminated at a particular point in my life where I knew that exploring the why behind my distorted behaviour would help me, and others who might be living a similar story, relearn how to attain the glory and beauty of love that God intended.

My journey started like any pubescent childhood fascination. My body was changing and so were the girls around me. New thoughts and feelings started to develop, and I was intrigued to explore them more. Over time my childlike inquisitive nature grew into a flourishing beast of a man, eventually weighing heavily on me in the years that followed. Porn ruined me in a lot of ways. It kept me from self-belief and from confidence in who I was or who I could be, leaving me instead with emotional larceny. Even while writing this book it still haunted me. Amid finding the right words, emotions spilled out like dirty laundry crammed in a teenager's closet. It wasn't so much the recollection and documenting of my childhood memories that made the whole writing process exhausting as it was the flurry of emotions that ensued days later.

Waves of anxiety pounded the weathered shoreline of my mind. I remember waking up in a cold sweat one night, recalling the vivid dream I had. I could see my brain covered in thick, coagulated tar, like a smoker's lung. I struggled to form any words to call out for help as my thoughts were caked in a smoky residue, and I floundered through a fog of indecision. Although I was aware of the residual build-up, a part of me knew the diagnosis was favourably reversible. As I stumbled on, I soon felt a refreshing gust of wind that wrapped around the back of my head, sending shivers down my neck. The tar started to crack, eventually peeling away, and the dense haze soon dissipated. That's when I woke.

A huge part of writing this is that I never had the luxury of reading something by someone who asked and wrestled with the same questions I had. I scoured bookshelves and online sites. I took courses and read literature. These resources were certainly helpful, but they lacked the authenticity I craved. Something about them just didn't grip me, didn't win me over completely. Most of the content was delivered by guys who sounded like youth pastors telling you to not date, yet who were never in relationships themselves. You can relate, right? Although wisdom can come without experience (to a degree), you will always lack a certain sense of street-smart credibility. There was nothing I found to be relatable: a man or woman shedding light on how their distorted view on sex rendered them incapable of love. There are hundreds of books on how to be pure and how to 'walk the walk' and be a good, godly man. I needed more—conversation, for starters, like the way Jerry pontificates with George at Monk's Café. The jesting and jousting between two people getting the complicated idiosyncrasies of life off their chest in an authentic way. The stuff I did find felt like a forced conversation your dad would have had with you when you were a teenager. I don't want this book to come across as flippant, but I sincerely hope it's as warm as receiving a friend's advice. The only person I have seen address lust and love in an honest way on a grand scale is the notorious Russell Brand. I'm not a huge fan of his verbose usage of cockney adjectives, but he strikes a chord that's always relatable. As a past serial womaniser, he too has struggled with his fair share of demons, and for someone who appears erratic, he rants on the gravity of his sexual vices: 'Our attitudes towards sex have become warped and perverted and have deviated from its true function as an expression of love and a means for procreation. Because our acculturation—the way we've designed it and expressed it—has become really, really confused.'[1]

Interestingly, Brand says that if he had total dominion over himself, he would never look at pornography again. What I love about this honest admission is that it highlights two fundamental things. First, he recognises the need to relinquish any control he might assume. Technically, he has none. It's an addiction issue more significant than himself and his strength. The second point is that he uses the word *again*. Now, this might be an assumption on my behalf, but it implies that he's not completely free, that it's a continuous fight. As with any shift in mindset, he humbly acknowledges the work he must put in every single day. What he says isn't compelling because it's coming from Russell Brand (well, maybe a little) but because he's telling his audience the way it is. He's vulnerable and bare, emptying his pockets of any hidden mistruths. People love and respect that kind of honesty. It's in our human nature to gravitate towards those who have suffered through similar experiences. Just look at war movies. Platoon members call each other brothers because it's the closest bond one can get. Why? They've been through some horrific ordeals and share unique experiences. It's the reason Russell's comments are so powerful. He's clearly in the midst of his own mental war, but his first win is his admission to take full ownership.

People always trust someone who's walked the

talk. It's why Jesus was so appealing in his day—and still is. There's a reason for his incarnation. He arrived as a man and he suffered as we do. He was also tempted beyond belief, more so than the average person. So when Jesus speaks of temptation, when he uses parables to illustrate trials and tribulation, he's speaking not only on behalf of the Father above but right from the heart, from his flesh and bone—one reason why the communal bread and wine today represent his flesh and wounds. It's a reminder that he was human and suffered, that he bore all our sins and overcame. And in his strength, we can too. I'm no different from millions of people out there with a similar cross to bear. I'm not special, and I claim no superpower. The only difference is that I have chosen to openly write about a subject often too demonising for most to talk about. It's not a self-help book, but an exploration I've wished to share for years, despite days when it seemed impossible to even begin. This book took a certain amount of risk, and my wife began to be more supportive of me not only while writing it but in overcoming a lot of issues in the process. She would ask what I hoped to achieve by throwing down the gauntlet to my intimate thoughts—not as a loaded question but as a way to get me to distil what I wanted to convey.

My knowledge and authority is my experience. All I have to impart are useful bits of information I amassed along the way, like a fervent squirrel gathering nuts for winter. It's here for you to take from it what you can, like a rusty toolbox full of utilitarian possibility, in a shed. As Russell Brand puts it in his Essex twang, 'If you're constantly bombarded with great waves of filth, it's really difficult to remain connected to the truth.' So to answer my wife, if you really want to hear the truth and understand this 'thing' that offends you and robs you of intimacy, then read on. If nothing else, I hope you learn to rethink love and unlearn lust. Then my odd ramblings will finally have meant something, without sounding too 'pulpity'.

Enjoy.

THE SUBJECT OF OBJECTIVITY

AT AROUND 3:30 A.M. ON A CRISP JANUARY MORNING, a Toyota Supra was casually meandering down Interstate 75 in Detroit when it suddenly careered off the road, crashed, and rolled, partially ejecting the driver through the sunroof, instantly ending his life. When Michigan State Troopers arrived on the scene, the man's death was marked by apparent ignominies. Oddly, his trousers were unbuckled, and when the officers recovered his damaged mobile phone some distance from him, they discovered adult content he had clearly been watching while driving. It seemed he had lost control of many things that night. I was easily allured by this clickbait article while flicking through my social feed, particularly because the headline read, 'Death on the Road, Porn on the Phone.'[1] It wasn't so much the farcical nature of the story that grabbed my interest as much as the evidence to a backstory much bigger than a night-time 'joyride.' As the article's author suggests, 'At first sight, his last drive was all about sex, but I think it was despair, not lust, which killed him.'[2] I'm certain that this story would've begged for double entendre in other tabloids, but for this journalist there were more questions than why the driver was caught with his pants down. Sexual gratification was merely surface level. What led the driver down this empty road? What was in his rear-view mirror that he was desperately trying to shake off and leave behind? Loneliness? Despair? Guilt? Who knows? But anyone reading between the lines would feel that in a cruel way he succeeded, albeit in a grim and unplanned way. The journalist concludes with a fitting quote by his irreverent gonzo counterpart, Hunter S. Thompson: 'He who makes a beast of himself gets rid of the pain of being a man.'[3]

This story of hopelessness driving a man to escape the overwhelming isn't unique; what is unique is how he died. The real tragedy was the shameful way in which it played out that evening, sadly making it newsworthy. The article initially saddened me, but as I read on further in the comments below, I became increasingly annoyed. Perhaps in my naïveté I expected some display of sympathy, but I found none. Only an indelicate mass response that fuelled my frustration. I tried to persuade myself to lighten up. I even assured myself that it's what trolls do best on a newspaper's Facebook feed. They don't truly reflect the genuine readership of the paper. They couldn't possibly. But I was wrong. The thread had birthed an ongoing pun-fest, long on witty rebuttals and short on compassion. Despite feeling saddened for the driver, the vitriol made me even sadder. I was embarrassed for humanity. The jesting and jousting had led people to glaze over the author's true intent. I realised that laughing off an awkward topic helps to avoid the subject altogether. It's what we do best when we don't know what to say at all. Try to get a serious word in amongst the boisterous cackles in a sex ed class, and you'll know exactly what I mean.

In truth, I shouldn't have been surprised at the comments. Thousands of stories like this are being passed over every day. Luckily for some, not all are made public, but when exposed intentionally or unintentionally, the world's response is nothing less than the attitude of this article's readers. The shameful reality is that any other confronting subject would receive quite the opposite. Had the driver had one hand on the steering wheel and another clutching a can of beer instead, I hardly think the responses would've been equally laughable. More likely, there would have been collective outrage:

"What if he had killed someone?"

"He's clearly an alcoholic."

"Somebody should've stopped him."

More colourful words probably were used, but you get my point. The problem with any addiction is that it's not a simple A-to-B drop-off and, 'thanks for the ride.' It can be never-ending, where one turn leads to another twist and then another, similar to the classic Choose Your Own Adventure books. As a kid I loved how my choices would inevitably influence the story arc, the risk versus reward. I couldn't wait to finally make it to the end of the chapter and experience the excitement of reaching the choice of two numbers at the bottom of the page. 'If you decide to look inside the treasure chest, turn to page 88. Or, should you choose to alert Detective Chimes about the bizarre discovery you found, turn to page 123.' This curiosity stirred an eagerness to keep going on, leaving me perched on a cliff and determined to find out what would happen next. It was the same rush of excitement I would experience years later at the birth of my own addiction. When I read the *Guardian* article, I felt overwhelmed with empathy because I shared a similar struggle I was so desperate to leave behind—an addiction that tortured me for years. I've since numbed to the residual effects. Even now as I knock out the letters on the keyboard, part of me feels slightly cavalier and fraudulent because the struggle never seems finite. I'm aware of my flaws and the fact that pride becomes your closest ally when the rest of the world can be heard laughing at you.

I suppose that just like the apathetic responses to the article, part of me shrugs it off as a monkey on my back that's lived with me all my life. At first it was nothing more than mischievous curiosity, the excited gibber in my ear nudging me to explore something new. As the years progressed, the innocent playfulness turned to heavy pounding of fists. And as the monkey grew, my pubescent exuberance quickly transpired into a heavy-footed, shoulder-slumped, knuckle-dragging swagger. The more I lived with it, the more it weighed me down. Eventually the burden became unbearable, and it was easier to take a seat. Sitting became a regular stance for my sloth-like slumber: idle, weak, and alone.

Sexual addiction is far more elusive than other vices. In the beginning, the signs aren't as visible. It's not like smoking a cigarette in the school toilets and hosing yourself down with a cheap can of deodorant. No matter how hard you try, it seeps into the fabric of your soul. It might be odourless to you, but eventually the overwhelming smell will call you out. The signs gradually appeared years later, like well-worn shoes, accustomed but oblivious to the stitching coming undone. Only now when I chronologically trace my steps am I able to distinguish between the subtlety and severity, though I would struggle to tell you what's more perverse, my objectification or complacent acceptance. The more I allowed my sexual curiosity to meander, the more I yielded. Before I knew it, I had drifted into fifth gear without recalling the shifts in between.

I'm aware that I casually throw around the term *sexual addiction* a lot, but I struggle to define it without being widely categorical. Sexual addiction is more universally recognised, yet it has always sounded to me like some seedy penchant for ladies of the night. Perhaps unwanted sexual behaviour might be a better descriptor. I never was on a hunt for physical intimacy, nor was I solely obsessed with pornography, where every tab on my computer was a rabbit hole to Wonderland. I was undoubtedly addicted, but it felt more like a lustful chastity: an insatiable hunger which kept me chained to an obsession, impossible to shake. Lust can mean many things. There's lust for power, or fame, or sexual gluttony. When I think of this word *chastity*, I think of someone being locked up in chains, like in the scene from *Return of the Jedi* where Princess Leia is in her iconic metal bikini slave costume—chained and collar-bound for eternity by her captor, Jabba the Hutt (nothing beats a relatable analogy like *Star Wars*, but I digress). You could say that my experience was similar: bound against my will by an overbearing monster. As the years passed, the hold on me got stronger and tighter. Like any addiction, if you don't get a handle on it sooner, it's harder to rein it in years later. Even though I may dwell on time lost, I can choose to exchange every lost minute for the wealth of knowledge gained.

Knowledge has helped me learn about myself and my affliction. To borrow the animated phrase of Uncle Ben to Spiderman, 'With great power comes great responsibility.' In my case, knowledge replaces power. The difficulty for most men is the constant wrestling with a warped misconception over what feels natural and true versus an influx of deceptive misinterpretations and thoughts, an aphotic zone created by society. It's the reason we snigger in sex ed class or crack puns on social threads. We don't quite understand how to respond constructively. We experience a bodily function that feels natural and normal yet destructive at the same time: this compounds the mass confusion. What you're left with is men walking around in a weird, oxymoronic state, a disposition which overlaps and flows into a warped misunderstanding of women and otherwise. If men lack clarity, then how will their partners, sisters, mothers, and wives be equipped to help or offer any advice?

My casual abandonment of love instead of lust turned everything beautiful about the opposite sex into a dehumanised smorgasbord. I feasted on a whim. Being constantly bombarded with unrealistic, photoshopped, cheap imitations forced me to lose any authentic connection with girls. It took me years to see women as a sacred gift from God who bear the image of Christ—the absolute mark of beauty. Can you imagine hearing these words in your sex ed class? I can't say it was a quick and easy conclusion for me. I had to unlearn everything with which I had filled my mind. If you go back to Genesis, the original sin plays out this demise. Adam and Eve—both gifts from God, in his likeness and made for unity—see each other as beauty reflected by God, whole and complete. When they gaze at one another, they see a familiar being designed to give and receive love. But we know the story doesn't end there. The moment sin enters the garden, they lose their ability to comprehend one another as complete goodness. In an instant, all they see is flesh, an image laid bare, a body reduced to nakedness. We've built an entertainment industry on looks first, character last. Shows like *Married at First Sight, Naked Dating, Body Makeover, Seven Year Itch, Love Island*, and otherwise. Could you ever imagine watching a show called *Inner Beauty Island*? The world has placed importance on looks and given it precedence over anything else. Your worth is now based on your beauty. Facebook, a billion-dollar company, originally started as a hot or not list for college girls.

I could never overcome my lustful thoughts. My attrition was always slow-moving, filled with little wins rather than immediate victory. I say slow because there wasn't some 'ta-da' moment for me. I always knew the truth, mindful of the daily guilt and years of affliction I carried with me. My fighting skills were shaky and my defences reactive and ill-equipped. Like a child, I would learn from every foolish mistake I made instead of thinking through the consequences first. I had no master trainer, no red-faced coach yelling at me from the sidelines, flapping his arms commanding me in one direction or the other. I was directionless and self-taught. I tried to fight back but would eventually wane and tire.

———

Many of you may have a similar backstory to the driver on Interstate 75. You feel as though you've travelled a similar proverbial road, making the same loop over and over again. Stopping to ask for help doesn't feel like an option for fear of being judged, and understandably so. There's no enticing invitation to simply open up. Going public only feels like ammunition to be scoffed at. And the safest of places—the homes; the bedrooms; the arms of a loving spouse, girlfriend, or even parent— aren't as welcoming as we hope them to be. At least we don't trust them to be. The more we hide in shame, the more we allow our battle to be labelled as a dirty little secret, the more we are backed into a corner and the more we give power to sin's control.

The truth is that the driver didn't have to travel alone. And neither do we. We don't have to be haunted by our reflection. The more we educate ourselves and others, the easier it will be to talk openly. I truly believe it's the reason why men laugh it off amongst other men and why a majority of women are misinformed. We have to break this stigma and flippancy about the subject. This common objectification is swept aside far too easily. Trust has been abandoned, feelings have been hurt, and lives are being ruined. The comments in the *Guardian* article are proof as to why I want to tackle this subject. It's what I hope to achieve with this book, whether you are a man or a woman reading it—that we all start the conversation, with men talking openly to other men, husbands talking to wives, women initiating conversations; that it's okay to rebuke the act constructively instead of laughing at the friend or partner who struggles with it; that instead of posting sexual puns, we would share our own experiences and encourage others in their journey. Only then will we win this battle, and spouses, armed with knowledge, will help their wounded partners fight on.

Lust

When we lust after cheap imitations of true beauty, we lose the ability to have real connections. Quitting sounds a lot easier than it really is, especially in a world where we're bombarded with unrealistic representations. But it's more than simply quitting. The Bible calls us to 'pursue' righteousness and physically 'walk' in the spirit— both active verbs, clearly implying a daily mindset. It might seem tiring just thinking about it, but this is the Christian life, isn't it? It's a constant preparation of the mind, body, and soul. It's the antithesis of a lazy life, for lazy eyes are wandering eyes. The prize of not being governed by lust is to see one another in the fullness of our character and not simply reduced to an object for gratification. Equally, if you do find that your partner struggles with lust, you too can play a part in helping him or her lead a daily pursuit of righteousness, faith, love, and peace. Seek the knowledge you need through counsel or simply start the journey with a Google search. It'll only benefit the relationship in the long run. The first step in overcoming an addiction is not having to do it alone.

2

THE REALITY WITH FANTASY

*The more one sees of the other, the less one
would see the other.*

— PATRICK WILLIAMS

I REMEMBER A CHAT I ONCE HAD WITH A FRIEND,
Trevor, from Ireland. He's always been a good mate,
different from all the others in that I like the way in
which he thinks about life. Being a mathematician, he's
incredibly smart and often sees the world through the
lens of pragmatism and logic. Existentialism is never
really on the catch-up-over-a-pint agenda. Ironically,
his opinion on life matters tends to be Kierkegaardian:
black-and-white, either-or. This particular conversation
was about women. It all started with a bold statement
that could also pass for a gross generalisation. It was
the type of one-liner you rarely forget and at some

point in your life will gladly pay forward in conversation.

"D'you know why dem ladies like dem TV soaps?" he said, tinged with a thick plummy Cavan brogue.

He paused, the same way one expectedly waits at the end of a knock-knock joke. I half-heartedly humoured him.

"Why?"

"Because dey love drama; it's why dey always love to fight wit us."

"Us?" I nudged.

"Any fella in a relationship."

He leaned back into his chair, somehow relieved to have shared this sensational scoop. As absurd as it sounded, I wasn't quick to write him off, because many of his observations on life, particularly his philosophy on love, weren't always his own original notions. A lot of his inside information was usually lost in translation, making its way from the source of authorship—his fiancé. She's lovely, but she's fervently leftist: anything to do with atheism, feminism, and the marginally repressed, and she's all over it like a trending Twitter hashtag. So I am judicious with Trevor's worldview at times.

I remember my ex-girlfriend once told me she really needed to fight with me. She wanted to argue, which is an odd thing to admit to someone. Why the heck would anyone want to argue? It made no sense and seemed counterproductive. However, she knew how to goad me, like a horse whisperer with a bronco. Except it had the reverse effect. The more I thought about her comment, the more annoyed I got. I was angry. She had already won! Truthfully, I can't recall what the fight ended up being about, but I saw a glimpse of truth in Trevor's initial theory—well his fiancé's, though, grossly generalised from Trevor.

What she originally implied is that women thrive off passion. It's what fuels them. We might call it drama, but the connotations are different. The reason most men feel like their partners are all up in their grill is because there's a need for an awakening of something real, raw, and energised. It's why a man's ardent stance is attractive. I know my wife doesn't want me to be a 'yes dear, no dear' husband. All she needs is confident reassurance from time to time that I'm fit and motivated to be a part of the team. Men, on the other hand, generally prefer to distract themselves until the problem goes away. We're less connected to our emotions. We'd much rather command a legion of orcs on Xbox than concern ourselves with the fact that Susan isn't talking to Trish. And despite the latter appearing trivial, it's far more real than the make-believe world we seem to embrace. I remember when I was a kid I watched *MacGyver* every Friday night. Come Saturday morning I was him. There I'd be out in the garden toying with my Swiss Army knife pretending to make the wildest contraption out of a piece of flint and fishing line. Van Damme was another.

You remember the famous scene where he kicks the bamboo shoot in a controlled meditative move until his shins bleed? I'd impersonate him by training for revenge against my 'brother's death' on my mother's flourishing hydrangea bush. Short on bamboo, I'd hack it like a crude cutting machete. Not very Zen, still. That said, if we had it our way we'd avoid our real lives as much as possible.

Everybody loves to dream big and let their mind wander to the fantastic. In my opinion, somewhat generalised, there seems to be a distinction between a man and a woman's idea of fantasy. A man seems to be lured more easily, where one rabbit hole leads to another, whereas a woman appears to be far more tuned to here and now, less easily lured by fantasy gimmicks. In other words, she seems less manipulated into always needing to 'escape.' Cautious of not letting speculation blur facts, I discovered some interesting insights into the male obsession with fantasy tribes. The gaming advocacy group ESA (Entertainment Software Association) compiled a report in 2016 stating that the median age and gender of a video gamer is a thirty-five-year-old male. On average, 59 per cent of the gender of game players is male and only 41 per cent is female.[1] If we turn to fantasy sports, according to the FSTA (Fantasy Sports Trade Association) the average age is thirty-eight years old—again, predominantly male. In 1988 there were 500,000 players in fantasy sports leagues. Today there are over 59.3 million and roughly 71 per cent are male.[2] The same can be said for online gambling. According to the Statistics Portal, the market volume of the online gambling industry was forecasted to reach USD 51.96 billion in 2018, more than doubling since 2009.[3] And, no surprise, it's predominantly male. It's never been easier to pick up your phone and throw fifty dollars at your team's chances of winning.

My point is that there's this invisible line woven into us from an early age, right through to adulthood. This common thread links our fascination with fantasy worlds and a desire to find something new and entertaining. And if you trace this thread to its source, you'll discover how it slowly unravels a game of objectification. So I get why most men fall into the seduction of something like porn at an early age and then struggle to shake it their whole life. It evolves and caters to many different desires. The problem with sexual fantasy is that it can often blur the lines of reality.

I remember times when I would wake, unable to tell the difference between what was real and what was make-believe. It was as if I lived in one world more than the other. There were nights when I would spend my whole evening living in this world. Nothing outside would matter. I wouldn't respond to texts, emails, or a phone call. My daily moments of escape became better than what the outside world had to offer. It sounds messed up, but it's how it was for me. If I had a bad day at work, I knew I could always come home and find solace in a world where I was king, where I could dictate how things would play out and make me feel. It was a place where I could be whomever I wanted to be, with whomever, depending on how I wanted to feel. I could forget about the bills, my workload, problems with friends and sneak off to my quiet, happy place. Although I knew it was unnatural, it did feel as normal as watching a movie or playing video games. In fact, I didn't feel any different from the video game addict who stays up all night trying to level up. Fantasy had become a paradox for me. It's beautiful to fill your mind with wonder and imagination, but it can also be used as a crutch for avoiding life.

This notion of living another life, where you can dip into a parallel universe, bombards us daily. Noise is all around us, vying for our attention. During my years in the advertising industry, my role was to think up new ideas to help clients sell a better way of life: Just another thing you needed to feel complete. It didn't take long for my work to become a conflict of interest. Although I needed the paycheque and deceived myself into believing the commercials I wrote were an artistic form of entertainment, I was lying to the world, including myself. I was playing God, selling miracles and marvels, convincing the masses that their lives wouldn't suck as much if they would only eat a certain type of cereal every morning. I played on people's need for a sense of direction and affirmation. It's that easy. All you have to do is walk around your neighbourhood and you'll see houses filled with juicers, flat screens, and an ab cruncher, all promising a better life.

This searching for something else, this desire to fill a void, is no different from pursuing things like porn and drugs. Granted, there are degrees of harm, but it all leads to a common desire to escape, no matter how you dress it up. We've just labelled some things as more normal than others, when truthfully, it's nothing more than semantics.

Over the last decade, reality TV has skyrocketed to new heights. This idea of watching real life unfurl in our living rooms, in its raw and uncompromising nature, is now the new way of entertaining—our fix for something authentic. The irony is, there's nothing accessible about any of these shows today. It is life subtly manipulated, recreated, lacking any credibility. Yet we're still lured by the nature of gossip, drama, tragedy, and love. We attach ourselves to the characters, believing them to be real, identifying with the lifestyle they're feeding us. We're led to believe that the protagonists are raw and unyielding, even if their setting is fantastical. Producers know that if the characters are seen as frauds, the audience will have been lost. They have become masters at making it increasingly impossible to tell what's written and what's genuinely off-the-cuff.

My experience with lust felt like this. I constantly struggled with differentiating between the person, the environment, and the performance. For instance, a sexy billboard of a girl in underwear, albeit against the backdrop of a set, would appear fantastically real for me. Let me break down my thought process. The environment, whether a setting on a pirate ship or in front of a photographer's infinity curve, is the fantasy element. The subject in front of the lens is the real element, despite the character portrayed. And the performance is a subtle stand somewhere between the two. If convincing and enticing enough, it'll appear true. It's the sweet spot on a spirit level. When I've spoken with men, even some women, about sexually provocative imagery, I'm usually met with the same response. They will dismiss it as nothing more than fantasy, a reoccurring rebuttal that I find implausible. If it's 'just' fantasy, then why is it being presented as something real? If it's 'just' fantasy, why do men keep returning to porn sites looking for something tangible and real? Surely the only fantasy component is the act of escaping. Everything else is real. Despite the nondescript label of *adult entertainment* and bad acting, the sexual performances are still genuine. Football is a beautiful game, but just because it's a form of entertainment doesn't make the skill in scoring a goal any less real. The girl in the strip club is very real. She might be dancing seductively and performing a set routine, but she's still someone's daughter. She has a mother and a father. Perhaps she's even a wife or mother. Her title *stripper* isn't who she is. It isn't what truly defines her. It's a persona, a character, a title, but a very real person is behind all of it.

I'm not dismissing the role of fantasy as a whole; it exists, but it's always brought to life by a real entity. A dose of reality is, after all, woven into the fabric of fantasy. My point is this: when intimate moments between two people are staged in a very heightened fantasy in front of a very real audience, the line between fact and fiction blurs and plays tricks on the mind.

There's a reason shows like *The Bachelor* and apps like Tinder are all the rage, setting the Twitter-sphere ablaze. Neither one of them is a true representation of reality, despite their best efforts at appearing so. *The Bachelor* is a constructed, hyper-real environment where a woman's worth is based on a thornless rose from a man who has cherry-picked them from an assorted box of ladies who are eventually cast aside like crumpled wrappers. I have a name for this notion of ordering a perfectly assembled package of love: fast food romance. The same can be said for the Tinder app. A friend at work recently asked me to have a look at all the girls who had contacted him and to tell him whether I thought any of them were good enough to 'hit up.' He had never reached out to them; they reached out to him. He had thirty hits, jabs, pokes, winks, nudges, likes, whatever you want to call it. And for some reason he roped me in to help solve his problem. There I was, reclined in my work chair, picking through these girls like marked-down clothes on a sale rack. "No, no, no . . . possibly . . . hmmm . . . I'll come back to this . . . interesting . . . definitely not," and on it would go. I did it only to amuse him and partly myself, but it left me feeling as cheap as the girl I was casually swiping left. I admit I got carried away with the novelty of this fleeting fantasy. At first it was exciting and mysterious, soon followed by feelings of disillusionment and sorrow. I never bothered reading anyone's bio. I did exactly what everyone else does on the app: I judged whether they were hot. I eventually handed the phone back to him, narrowing my selections to a conservative three. He opened each gallery and stolidly flicked through my shortlist like a discarded pile of Joker cards. I realised I had only looked at their cover photo and not the pictures in their gallery. I had clearly made a rookie mistake. "Nah," he rattled, "look at this photo, too fat, too weird, and what does she think she's doing in this?" he protested. I wasn't seeing what he was. All this swiping left and right was confusing.

I asked him if he was planning on contacting any of the selected few, especially the one girl who gave him a 'wink' every month.

"I don't ever plan to mate, don't see the point," he dismissed.

"So why are you even on then?" I said, confused.

"Not sure, just a bit of fun to have a look-see," he brushed aside.

It was as though he loved the affirmation: the winks telling him he's okay, that he still has it, whatever 'it' was. What initially seemed to be a playful exercise felt like a pointless one. I rolled my chair back to my desk opposite his and sat at my computer, my mind flooded with more questions than answers. Beyond the app's frivolity and gamification, I realised that a lot of people out there are looking for something in a make-believe world, some sort of hope to hold on to. Despite the promise of an easier solution to life's problems, many of these apps pull us farther apart from one another. They don't help us discover more, talk more, delve deeper, or build long-lasting relationships. It's all surface-level stuff, like romantic takeaway where we never have to think about what's on the plate in front of us.

If marriage has taught me anything, it's that true love welcomes the day in well-worn pyjamas and the cologne of morning breath. You would assume that the more time spent in your partner's company, the less the candle of delight flickers and burns. It's the case for some relationships, but not all. We all have a choice as to how we value someone. Either they become nothing more than an object, or we cultivate the ability to push on through to find true beauty in the whole, not in an amalgam of parts. Fantasy isn't sustainable. It's why one escapes to it but never stays. It's fleeting, like the initial stages of newfound love. It's exciting but is too infant to bear any substance.

I'm reminded of a scene from the movie *Dan in Real Life*, featuring Steve Carell. The story is a confronting, impartial look into family dynamics and romantic love. In one scene between Dan and his daughter, they have a heated argument about her new holiday romance. She protests like one in a Shakespearean love tragedy, but her father shuts down any notion of budding true love. He's insistent that infatuation and sexual attraction isn't true love. Eventually, through the conviction of the nescient boyfriend, Dan acknowledges that love isn't a feeling but an ability. I'd go as far as to say that love isn't a feeling; it's a choice. It sounds callous, but I strongly believe it to be true. When all expectations and lofty feelings settle, true love rises up. You don't need butterflies to sustain it (maybe in the initial stages, for chemistry, but we all know the lifespan of a butterfly). Such a feeling isn't long-lived. The love of a brother doesn't require me to feel a giddy fluttering before I'm willing to drop everything and be there for him in his most desperate time. It's not romantic, but neither is it guaranteed just because it's family. Love can be effortless and equally an effort. It's all part and parcel of living in a very real world, a world that can be unforgiving at times but where true beauty lives. A place you don't need to escape to or from.

Fantasy

It took me many years to realise that fantasy exists only when we make a choice not to step with it into reality. I take no issue with fantasy. I believe it to be healthy to a point of inspiring and sustaining creativity. While it may invoke passion and a new zest for life, it can also be used as a familiar escape mechanism. A preoccupation with fantasies of immeasurable power, success, intellect, beauty, or absolute love can do more harm than good. Adopting it as a way out of dealing with real problems only exacerbates them even more. Pornography, for instance, is often argued as being a way to invigorate one's sex life through fantasy. I would argue that its addictive nature exaggerates a perception of sexuality in society—and is anything but real. Like all addictions, sexual addiction thrives in an unrealistic world; it distorts the spontaneous nature of love (warts and all). For some, their partners suffer from a disposition known as fantasy-prone personality—their fantasy world has hijacked their real world, making it impossible to distinguish between the two. Others simply describe this type of person as a daydreamer or 'fantasiser.' If you notice that your partner struggles with being present, often needing time alone to escape, then consider it as an early warning sign. Helping your partner become more present, living in the now, will have its challenges. It won't be instantaneous, but if they are to start truly appreciating the real joy this life has to offer, it starts with an understanding of why they tend to escape from it in the first place.

3

I NEVER KISSED DATING GOODBYE

*Young men's love lies not truly in their hearts,
but in their eyes.*

— WILLIAM SHAKESPEARE

SMACK BANG IN THE MIDDLE OF PICCADILLY CIRCUS'S
famous traffic intersection sits a memorial fountain
where thousands gather each day, using it as a meeting
point, a focal point for photos, or as a spot to take a
breather from the exhausting high street shopping.
Perched above the fountain leans a statue of a half-
clothed messenger boy with a bow and arrow. Most
tourists think it's Cupid, while Londoners know it as
Eros, the Greek god of sensual desire and love. I admit
the first time I saw it, it looked a lot like the beneficent
angel who fires arrows at unsuspecting couples,
inspiring love and romance in every victim. In fact, this

statue is neither about love at first sight nor about Eros, as we're led to believe. Rather, it is about his twin brother, Anteros, the ancient Greek symbol of selfless love, erected in honour of Lord Shaftesbury's charitable life as a dedicated campaigner who fought against many injustices like slavery, child labour, child employment, and child prostitution, to name a few.

What strikes me most about common misperceptions is that, like the tourists, I too was mistaken by the image of love. I grew up thinking it was something you desired and received - I need to be loved, who can I find to love me. Yes, of course, I also considered it as something you showed towards someone, but never as an Anteros type of love or what Christians would refer to as an *agape* love: a selfless love despite reciprocity. Only years later, when I married my wife, did I learn that true love isn't about what I can get, but about what I can give unconditionally.

Most of my childhood was confusing. Home was a shelter from the harsher and less desirable aspects of childhood. I grew up with a tremendous amount of anxiety, especially when it came to girls. I always felt like a late adopter, playing catch-up to whatever 'hooking up' buzzword was being thrown around the school playground. Figuring out what each 'base' meant was as foreign as the rules of cricket to an

American. As for my confidence, it waned as I was increasingly segregated based on my hair colour. Some mornings I was greeted as 'Step-hen' and other times as 'carrot top' (despite the obvious comeback that a carrot's top was, in fact, green). My hair wasn't fire truck red, cherry brown, or crimson, which meant that I experienced less vitriol than my other ginger brothers.

My assessment of where I placed on the social barometer was somewhere in the middle. I was never picked first for things, nor last. So it felt normal to only kiss a girl halfway through high school. My first girl-friend was at university. I thought I was doing all right. Girls seemed to like me, and pretty ones, too. It helped that I was funny. But I learned that making girls laugh was both a drawcard and a hindrance. People love a funny guy, but you'll always be seen as a joker. I seldom had the last laugh. Once I asked a girl I liked to the school dance. I was relieved when she said yes— until she added, "On one condition: as long as your friend Patrick is there." I had no idea about how dating actually worked. I know that no one really does, but I felt completely in the dark. 'Christian' dating wasn't any easier.

For most young adults, growing up in the church presents a shared fear of being single. I believe this feeling is more intense than for those who likely never grew up in the church. Even today as I scan various Christian blogs, this fear still exists. This sounds so flighty, but in 'church circles' it's unhealthily ampli-fied. For some unknown reason, singledom seems to plague young Christians' minds to the point that they feel like lepers if they're not hitched. This junction between God and finding 'the one' has become obses-sive. It interrupts every thought. Every single young Christian, somewhere, is secretly doing a reconnais-sance mission, scouring the prospective Pentecostal terrain. It's what I used to do. I would often sit at the back of church, imagining the possibility that God would summon a girl to serendipitously cross my path at some point between the close of worship and packing up. Every Sunday night I would shuffle back to the car, fruitless and head down. I'd drive home spouting some theological monologue, justifying my loss as God's leading me to a higher calling. Girls were obviously an unnecessary distraction. As deluded as I was, this provocative exaggeration numbed my anxiety. Despite taking comfort in the company of fellow single brothers, it didn't quell the desire, nor did it make attending Christian outings any easier. I would try my hardest to avoid couples who clung sickeningly to one another so as not to jinx the will of God and be forced apart. I'm sure you think this is either naively sweet or nauseatingly cringeworthy. The truth is, it was then and still is very real for young Christians. You have only to look at young people's reading choices on their bedside tables or scan the hundreds of blogs lamenting their relationship dilemmas. Knowing what I know now, I wish the older me could've told the younger me that I was wasting my valuable time worrying about all this. I would've told my youth pastors to discuss it more because it never was—ever. Young people worry about this kind of thing every waking hour. You're either in the club or you're out of the club, and if you feel left out, you just can't seem to get past it. It stays with you throughout your twenties, and the more it stays with you, the more it eats at you, and self-doubt starts to sink in. We're taught at a young age that to be whole we must be completed by someone else. Instinctively we have an internal desire to be partnered with some-one. We want a mate, and not just for beers and footy.

Although a relationship is a beautiful thing, it isn't what defines you—not when you're young, and certainly not when you're older. In fact, it never should. Finding a partner who 'completes you,' as Dr. Evil from *Austin Powers* would say, is a beautiful thing, but never in the sense where you should feel your life is finally complete and meaningful only once in a relationship. Part of the discovery of bringing two people together is a chemical and metaphysical concoc-tion of elation and terror at the same time. Two worlds colliding is never rudimentary. Self-awareness and affirmation come only through a concatenation of trial and error. Dating, after all, is much like fumbling in the dark. You will eventually find your bearings.

And there's nothing wrong with that. Despite many factions within the Christian community who believe otherwise, it isn't a sin. I'm conscious that many of you might have or still do practice this contentious school of thought: 'Kissing dating goodbye.' I shamefully raise my hand. I was one of the many introduced to Joshua Harris's book when it was all the rage as it made the rounds amongst small groups. If you're not familiar with it, you're not missing out. Well, technically you have missed the *love* boat because Mr Harris has since released a statement of regret on his website no longer agreeing with the central idea that dating should be avoided.[1] He's also discontinued its publication and every supplemental resource attached to it. It takes guts to put yourself out there and then admit that maybe you were wrong. I respect that. The lesson to be learned from all of this is that relationships are complicated enough without confusing young people any further. It's like trying to catch air with a net. It can't be sealed and packaged. It can be guided, sure, but it's tricky. Sadly, certain schools of thought in the church tried to push Harris's prescriptive agenda of courtship under supervision. While I understand the intended purpose of shepherding, imposing conservative views on impressionable young adults (who will follow just about anything that causes their hearts to flicker) is deeply dangerous. It does nothing more than create fear and confusion. I'm aware that this isn't everyone's experience. Some may have benefitted from applying some of the principles, but when practised as absolute gospel, it leaves very little to spontaneity and discovery.

I'm reminded of a time at Bible group when Pastor Squash and his wife spontaneously joined us for the evening. I was in university at the time, and our group would meet every Tuesday evening at a friend's house. I loved it because it was a chance to hang with like-minded people and shoot the mid-week breeze. I think that when you're young and entering new aspects of the world, trying to figure out who you are, linking to a group can be a comforting anchor. I remember having so many questions and new experiences, and I found value in chewing on them with a bunch of mates. It always helps to know that you're not the only one seeing the world as you do. So when our pastor and his wife dropped by, we were naturally excited. It's not often that you get to hang with the big dog in a small, intimate gathering where you can thrash out life's biggest questions.

I liked Pastor Squash. He was young and affable. I would only ever refer to him as 'Pastor Squash' around friends. I called him this because whenever new people visited the church, he would always ask if they played squash. If the answer was yes, he would volley an impromptu invite to a game at his local courts. Pastor

Squash was clever because his love for the game worked on two levels. It was a great way to recruit new visitors, and it also meant that he had your phone number, which was handy for data purposes. When I first visited his church, Pastor Squash tried his set piece move on me. Fortunately, a friend who had brought me along tipped me off. I told Pastor Squash that I wasn't very good and hardly played, and if he needed to reach me he could do so through my mate. My friend had fallen victim to Pastor Squash's power aces, but I didn't feel comfortable opening up with someone I had just met, especially not in a confined space over eleven points. Normally I would never commit the cardinal sin of lying to a pastor, but he was my age, so I suppose I felt bold enough to block the invite. Pastor Squash's wife was a lovely, gregarious American woman oozing the 'land of the free' spirit. They had married in their early twenties and moved to South Africa to start a church plant. She had initially come from a hugely popular Pentecostal church in the States led by a really well-known pastor in the local Christian community. Their ambition was to lay down the same blueprint that was so successful in her hometown. Sadly, a lot of the cultural nuances didn't translate well, and the church didn't last more than three years. The last I heard, they had been lured back to the States, where they both now work for her old church. They carried a one-size-fits-all methodology to everything they did, including their perspective on relationships.

On this particular evening at the Tuesday Bible study, Pastor Squash and his wife hoped to share their dating story. Perhaps they believed that giving an account of their own personal relationship history might help the group in their own pursuits. The story goes like this: he liked her, but he didn't act on his feelings until he heard from God. I can't remember the intricate details of whether she liked him, but let's just say that they had both been struck by cupid's love arrow. When he eventually got the green light from the Big Guy upstairs telling him that she was the one, it was all systems go. He didn't pursue her in the conventional kind of way that you or I might, but in the hey-let's-kinda-hangout way. A way where they behaved as faithful friends but with zero physicality. No kissing, no holding hands, nothing. The prescriptive 'I kissed dating goodbye' way.

While a part of me found this display of discipline admirable, another part of me found it deeply suspicious. Looking around the group it was clear they were hanging on his every word, like a day trader waiting for a buy signal. He concluded by stressing that after enough interaction, and only then, did he eventually pop the question. I suppose some would find this story magical and sweet, but it annoyed me, particularly when they smugly opposed any form of conventional dating. We 'singles' were to spend our time in the safety of groups as friends only, like some hippy commune. Until the clouds parted and a thunderous voice boomed in affirmation, then and only then would we have the cue to propose. It's hard not to be facetious when such a statement sounds so absurd. I didn't take issue with the particular way they approached relationships, but with how 'their way' was portrayed as the only way.

I sat there absorbing all that they had said, my mind on a spin cycle of confusion. I wasn't resistant to their message, but I struggled to comprehend the 'no dating, no kissing' policy they proudly plugged. I thoughtfully constructed my opinion while I waited for an opportune moment. The group seemed wide-eyed and receptive, but I couldn't wait any longer, so I piped up.

"May I quickly jump in . . . ?" Heads in the room turned with the synchronicity of a Wimbledon crowd. I continued, "Throughout my twenties, I dated a fair bit. All very different and all with their own set of nuances and life lessons. Some I regret, others I merely put down to life lessons, yet all of them were an education. I learned not only valuable relational skills but also a great deal about myself. In hindsight, it highlighted more of my flaws than those of the girls eating opposite me. Something I don't think I would trade for having held out."

There was a long pause. Evidently the words that spilled from my mouth had the same effect as tick bite paralysis. Any movement of facial muscles seemed sedentary, which made it somewhat ambiguous to read the room. The prolonged silence and awkwardness offered a hint. It became clear that Pastor Squash and his wife were stumped and surprised with my challenge to their prescription. As the pastor, he felt the need to defend his message, but it was evident there was some division in the room. What worked for them couldn't be the blueprint for all. It could never be. The algorithms of romantic encounters are by virtue incomprehensible. It's what makes them so beautiful and mysterious.

I remember leaving the meeting confused and angry. There were a few impressionable single friends in the group who I knew had clung to every word the pastor said. I was concerned that an honest discussion never surfaced that night out of fear of not having the answers in the first place, which would've been equally plausible. Instead, it opened up more questions than answers, eventually causing people to adopt an overly conservative approach.

I experienced this behaviour months later when I asked a girl, whom I had already established a good friendship with, out for coffee. For the record, my intention was only to hang out with her. Having grown up with only brothers, I welcomed the refreshing change of chatting with the opposite sex any chance I could get. I particularly enjoyed talking with her; she had a loud, infectious laugh that could wake a sleeping giant. So I was surprised when I was met with a resounding "No": "Sorry, Steve, I'd love to, but unless it's in a group setting there can't be any one-on-ones."

It was a common response. Not because I looked like the Elephant Man, but because for some reason it was deemed 'unwise.' While I attended this particular church, it had become the norm to kiss away any chance of hanging out with the girls. It wasn't only my experience; it happened to a lot of the guys there. I tried to use logic to understand.

"Okay, so how do I get to know you?" I would ask.

"Well, there's plenty of opportunities at church," they'd spout assuredly.

It was like saying to a hungry pride of lions, "Everyone, listen up! Before you delve into this zebra you've just brilliantly caught, could you all take a moment to group in single file and divide your share of the carcass equally? This way everyone gets the juicy bits, m'kay?"

Such a request would likely get your head bitten off. As much as I wanted to bite the head off of the next person who told me to enjoy the possibilities through group dynamics, I complied with an insincere smile. Admittedly, there are times when you are intrigued by a girl and want to see if there's anything more. Other times you want to be able to talk freely, far away from the post-church service chicory coffee. Sadly, I never got to know most of the girls beyond the pleasantries. The few I did never felt weirded out or pressured to prescribe to any Christian etiquette other than the obvious biblical basics. They felt comfortable enough to believe I wasn't going to slip Rohypnol into their caramel macchiato. The art of coffee with a splash of chat should feel entirely natural, and it did. There was no need for melodrama. This awkward relationship vortex would soon end when the church eventually did. Some would see the light, and others disappeared amidst the confusion. Thanks, Pastor Squash.

This one-size-fits-all approach to relationships is counterproductive, and fundamentalist rhetoric doesn't offer a sustainable solution any more than a bandage on a leaky faucet. While growing up, I longed to have some kind of help in navigating my way through all the questions and doubts bouncing around inside my head. Nothing I was hearing on a Sunday felt applicable to me. As a youngster, I spent my youth obsessing over 'finding the one' instead of finding myself. I was convinced that if I found my proverbial needle in a haystack, I would experience a perfect relationship of beautiful cross-stitch patterns. Unfortunately, life doesn't always weave so perfectly. There are no guarantees. Sometimes we might need to use duct tape to hold a snagged thread, other times we might need to sew until a pattern emerges. We might know its purpose only once things start taking shape, and even then, it might still come undone.

In my youthful malaise, I turned to what I thought relationships and women should be. It's how all my mates were getting knowledgeable. There were plenty of VHS tapes and worn magazines to go around. My eyes widened to a world which I used to view as narrow. I thought that this was how love was supposed to look and how we were to behave in relationships. I would give anything to go back in time and hear someone tell me that the beauty of love is not about finding the one, but about venturing through the mystery of life with the determination to come out the other side, differences and all, together.

Relationships

I wasn't looking for a 'how-to' manual on relationships growing up, because there was plenty of fluff out there already. I needed someone to tell me I'd be okay: a reassurance that my story would one day be unique and magical, not gospel for anyone else. Instead, I spent a good part of my childhood desperately trying to outsmart the romantic pontifications of the world in attempting to seek young love the 'right way.' I've yet to find a set of bullet points on dating in the Bible. If a union between a husband and wife is symbolic of God and the church, then surely the preparation and foundation of relationships between men and women should be an integral part of its agenda. The more we openly talk about it, the more we unveil an unnecessary mystery. We should encourage an environment where guys and girls alike can feel safe enough to hang together, have fun, and allow a situation to unfold naturally if informed wisely. Unnecessary sanctions on the heart are counter-productive, but we also shouldn't condone any form of sexual liberation outside of God's promise. Within the constructs of our relationship with Jesus, we should allow the many blessings of friendships between young men and women to flourish, to unfurl with common sense. I truly believe that if we develop a healthy mindset about the opposite sex from the outset, respect and understanding will improve and eventually lead to a healthy mindset on relationships. I wish somebody had told me earlier on to have fun, talk to girls, get to know them, date, and, most importantly, feel comfortable and confident without any agenda or legalism getting in the way. After all, there's enough pressure to make a lasting impression as it is.

4

THE EXPECTATION OF EXPECTING
TOO MUCH

*Only when it is dark enough can we see the
stars.*

— MARTIN LUTHER KING JR.

WHEN THINGS WERE GOING AWRY IN ONE OF MY relationships, my mother would always say, "Remember you're bringing two completely different worlds together. There's bound to be a clash of some sort." Although it sounded so obvious at the time, I never gave much thought to it until years later. She was right. No one can control how someone else thinks or feels about someone, and there will inevitably be a degree of uncertainty. Who can ever be 100 per cent certain? Yet we all tend to jump into every relationship the same way: head first and full of ideal expectations. If there's one relationship lesson I'm still learning,

even as a married man, it's this: unrealistic expectations will invariably leave you disappointed.

I once dated a girl who was a vegetarian. When I
met her I had no beef with eating meat. My favourite
pastime was making biltong (similar to jerky). As the
relationship progressed, I quickly became a male for
kale. You could say I was as much a vegetarian as
baseball's World Series involves the world. I thought
cutting out meat meant I could substitute it with pasta
dishes. Thankfully, she did most of the cooking which
was more balanced. One evening we were cooking
dinner at her apartment (something which involved
chickpeas, I honestly can't remember the dish). I had
just come back from a trip to Cape Town after visiting
a client with her ex-boyfriend (yes, you read that right),
and I was wrestling with something I wanted to bring
up at an opportune moment.

Now before I elaborate any further, it would help to
give some historical context. You could say that our
relationship started on an awkward footing. She had
come out of a long-term relationship, and I just so
happened to know her ex. Not only had I gone to the
same college as him, I also happened to work at the
same company. He had the face of Ivan Drago from
Rocky and a body that looked like it was constructed
from milk boxes, with organic egg cartons for abs. He
was a tank. When I asked him how often he went to the
gym, he told me twice a day, religiously. The only
thing I do twice a day with dedication is brush my

teeth. I'm not sure if his obsession for getting his pump on led to the demise of their relationship, but it certainly had an impact on ours. I tended to mould myself to impress. I would never transform completely, but I would always find a small crack to easily chip away at in the hope of securing my place. Sad, I know, but it took me a very long time to just be me.

It was rare that Mr Tank and I worked on a project together, but in this instance he just happened to be filling in for someone else. I can't remember if he was aware that I was dating his ex, but it was incredibly awkward for me. It was even more awkward sharing a hotel with him. I kept praying he wouldn't slam his massive fist into my face. It turned out that he was rather nice to me; in fact, he's always been really nice. But nice can also mask a lot of things. One night we had come back from being at a client meeting all day, and we headed to our rooms to turn in for the night. He had some work to do on his laptop, and I was making use of the free tea bags. He was sitting at the kitchen table trawling through some files when he called me over to look at something he thought might interest me. A grin stretched across his Ivan Drago jaw as he scrolled down a sequence of folders. At first I thought it might be some of the client's artwork that we could use for the project, but instead it was hundreds of chronological, archived folders of his favourite porn star. Each folder was labelled and packed with pics and clips. I hadn't been in any long-term relationships, so my ideas and expectations were often naive. Although I was dating his ex at the time, it took me by surprise how long he had been doing this, even while with her. The fact that his favourite porn stars were systematically stacked wasn't merely some post-breakup project. This was something he had carefully collected over the years. Yet here's a guy who, despite having a hot girlfriend and all the sex he wanted, was drawn to an obsession with heavy makeup, big busts, and awkward poses. I didn't get it. In my mind it wasn't how it was supposed to be. Only single guys look at porn, surely? But porn never discriminates. I would soon find this out.

Whenever I've been open enough to talk to girls about the topic of sex, especially when it comes to porn, I find there are two divided camps: Those who deny their partners have ever looked at porn, and those who admittedly find their partner's pornographic fix nothing more than harmless, passing fancy. One girl I know, who remains a good friend, used to buy her ex-boyfriend a *Hustler* magazine every month. It seems banal even when I write it down, but nowadays it would equate to an online subscription to a porn site. At the end of every month she would diligently pop to the newsagent after work and pick up the latest sealed issue for him to tear open. Why she was always the one to do it, I'm not entirely sure. Maybe he was embarrassed, or it was part of the kink. She, on the other hand, was nonplussed. It was no different to grabbing a carton of milk. When I asked her how she felt about it, she would shrug her shoulders and say, 'I get it, it's what guys do, they need to get off.'

While it was hard to argue with her, I still was shocked, perhaps even naive, to believe a loving partner would let themselves fall for such guff. Her passive response annoyed me. Her boyfriend's dirty secret had become as routine as getting his tighty-whities ironed by her every week. It didn't surprise me when their relationship finally ended. I don't think it was because of his monthly subscription in particular, but I'm positive it didn't help. It certainly didn't change her views in the slightest. There were times when her friends would randomly hand her a video of the latest porn movie for her and her new boyfriend to watch. Again, she was unexpectedly casual about it. She generously offered to lend it to me once they had 'finished' with it. Naturally, I retracted, though part of me was curious. My conscience nudged me. "No thanks, I'm good," I'd reply. My flesh would smile and whisper, "Don't worry, buddy; I'll find a way to sort you out later."

I remember the feeling of shame on the flight back home. Not because of what Mr Tank had shown me on his laptop, but because deep down I knew I would've been far more cavalier had he been a single guy instead of in a committed relationship. I wasn't sure if I could call it cheating, but I couldn't shake the feeling of betrayal for what he had done behind his then-girlfriend's back. And if I felt this way, then surely she would be horrified. You can imagine the irony I felt at the dinner table when I later broached this subject while passing a dish that was mostly made up of chickpeas.

"So, I saw something interesting while I was away," I said apprehensively.

"Oh yeah?"

"Yeah, Mr Tank randomly showed me something on his laptop."

"Why is it random?" she asked.

"Well, it's more *what* he showed me."

"And?" she nudged.

"And, well, it wasn't something I expected."

"Spit it out!" she insisted.

"It was porn."

"Porn?"

"Yeah, like lots of it."

She gently placed her fork face down, resting it on the edge of the plate. She buried her face into her napkin, and I watched as her two index fingers guided the end of the napkin around the sides of her mouth in what seemed to be the longest wipe.

"What do you mean by 'lots of it'?" she demanded.

"I mean, like a truckload." I held my hands out to approximate the hyperbole.

"I don't believe you."

"What?" I said in a strangled voice.

"You heard me!" she snapped back.

She jabbed, annoyed, one chickpea at a time with her fork, the same way someone eats a salad by prodding one green at a time. It irritated me; it's an insult to the iron age.

"Why would he show you?" she continued.

"I have no idea; he's probably proud."

"Proud of what?"

"His collection."

"You say it like it's some hobby."

"Well, he's clearly enthusiastic about it," I said smugly.

"But he knows you're dating me."

"Does he?" I asked, surprised.

"Yes, you . . . know . . . he . . . does." She hammered each word with precision.

I didn't really, but I wasn't going to question her for fear of adding further tension to an already strained conversation.

"Look," I cut in hard, "99 per cent of guys look at porn. It's a fact." (It's not a quantifiable fact; it's more a gut feeling. To be fair, many studies have shown that out of the number of sex addicts seeking help, 30 per cent are female. But I digress.)

She looked at me blankly. I continued.

"In fact, it's more than a fact. I've never met a guy who hasn't," I protested.

"Do you just randomly bring it up in conversation?" she snidely remarked.

"Why are you having a go at me?" I snapped. "I'm

just trying to educate you on the reality." And then lobbed a grenade. The sheer force was like a thousand chickpea shards knocking me off my chair.

"Do you look at porn?" She stared without blinking, her eyes refusing to miss a beat.

What are the chances she would believe I was the 1 per cent? My argument of potentially escaping had cornered me. Stuff it.

"All guys have at some stage," I deflected.

"You've angered me; I think you should go."

I was a little flummoxed. "Go? What have I done?" I objected.

How did this suddenly become about me? Indirectly, it was. I was no better than him. Even though I wasn't 'using' at the time, it was still dormant within me, ready to wake at any moment. She sat, arms folded in disbelief.

"It's too much for me to hear. I can't believe it. He never mentioned it to me. I never saw it. It just doesn't make any sense."

"I know. I don't want to upset you, but sometimes you guys need to be aware." In my attempt to defuse the situation, we butted up against my resolve like rubber ducks against an iceberg.

"What do you mean, 'you guys'?" she interjected.

"Well, I wish all women understood how seriously this affects guys."

"It's a lot to take in, Steve," she barked. "I feel hurt and betrayed, and yet you continue to generalise, 'this is what all guys do'. How do you expect me to react?"

I didn't say anything. It wasn't the time to throw back a smart aleck fact. I naively assumed it was apparent. Admittedly, I expected some shock, but it seemed too soon to try to enlighten her on the subject. And perhaps it was arrogant on my part for playing the conduit to shed light for all women in some attempt to exonerate all men. It backfired—badly. Her not 'getting it' annoyed me, and then she said something that infuriated me even more.

"I know him; he doesn't seem like the type of guy," she reasoned. "So I don't believe he was like this when we dated."

"Are you serious?" I verbalised in my head as my left eye twitched abnormally. I felt like shouting at her. But she was fragile. And I'm not stupid enough to joust. It would only end badly for both of us if I continued to hammer away. I tapered the conversation.

"I know what I have told you is hard to hear, and I can't say for certain that he was like this while you were dating, but it's possible."

She just stared into the distance. I wanted to explain how a lot of guys carry around this secret. I couldn't irrefutably prove it, the stats are there, but it was unintentionally an unspoken guy code. I was conscious of over-explaining and her misinterpreting my intention. Besides, all the stats in the world won't make any difference unless we talk openly. Sadly, this

is something we very rarely do. All we give is a
familiar smirk while we keep the truth hidden under a
mattress. Girls hide diaries there. Guys hide porn. I
didn't press her any further. I just sat there thinking
about similar conversations I've had in the past. I really
wanted her to understand, but I was also conscious of
the fact that I could come across as patronising.

Our relationship eventually passed on, along with my
phlegmatic temperament for meat. The real tragedy
wasn't the breakup, although that was also complicated; it was her sudden self-obsession to seek plastic
surgery—her adamant defiance that her happiness
depended on a few nips and tucks. It didn't matter that
I loved her for who she was, not what she looked like.
It was obvious and sad that she didn't care what I saw,
only what she thought everyone else could. In a cruel
way she had become the image of her own disbelief,
transforming herself into the girls in the glossy pictures
Mr Tank had hidden in his folders. She played into the
expectations of society—the same expectations that
fuel many men's addictive quest for ideal, unrealistic
women. She eventually got what she wanted: a life
reborn, without me in the picture. I never saw the final
result, only the bandages wrapped around her face and
body like some ribbon waiting to be unlaced. Even
though she's a past relationship I've deleted, I do hope

she allows someone to see the real her and not become another image on display filed in someone else's folder.

Expectations

There's enough social pressure as it is on who to be in the world and how to find success and happiness. The current vox populi across social media only fuels unnecessary and unrealistic expectations. It's a particularly disconcerting mindset for viewing relationships. Nowadays men and women feel a huge burden to not only live up to each other's expectations but also to demand them. There's a pressure to look a certain way, have a certain level of success, and even have sex a certain way. It's beginning to turn a generation of otherwise spontaneous, unique individuals into neurotic, obsessive overachievers. This is why I believe the most significant factor for divorce amongst young people today has to do with unrealistic expectation. There's no room for error, despite our beautifully flawed nature, warts and all. Porn is just one of the many facets that perpetuate these lofty tick boxes that are impossible to cross off. This is not to say we can't hope for the best in people, but when we expect it and it's unmet, it opens the door to unhealthy associations. Over the years I have been surprised by the many stories of friends and family who struggle with sexual addictions. And I've been equally surprised by the response of preconceived resentment and hurt. Sin is inevitably in all of us; we're flawed at birth. This is not to say that we should excuse our imperfections, but we can show grace and mercy to those we feel might have let us down. This book is not about justifying unwanted sexual thoughts and behaviour, but about showing how impartial it is and how many are plagued by it. If you have a warped view of sex, it will either manifest its way in the relationship or it will remain a dormant secret. The same is true with the opposite. If you expect your partner to have the same ideals of a relationship and sex as you do, only to discover the opposite to be true, you're more likely to be disappointed than understanding of their struggle.

5

WANDERING EYES

The eyes are the window to the soul.

— WILLIAM SHAKESPEARE

I'M SURE MOST OF YOU ARE FAMILIAR WITH MATTHEW 5:28, where Jesus speaks about lust. It's the most commonly referenced passage on this subject in the Bible: 'But I tell you that anyone who looks at a woman lustfully has already committed adultery with her in his heart' (NIVUK). It then goes on about the masochistic bit of plucking out eyes and chopping off hands. There have been times when I have seriously been tempted to do both. Even though I'm sane enough not to go to any extremes, I'm still frustrated and help-less. Whenever I have lusted, particularly while married, I've never for a second thought I committed adultery. If you had asked me if at the time it had crossed my mind, it would've seemed farcical. Perhaps I had talked myself out of any such notion, or maybe I never understood the true meaning of the words or power behind my actions.

Admittedly, a part of me couldn't comprehend lust of the eyes as cheating, because a large part of my gender group's eyes wanders at a very young age. And, for most kids, this could be sparked by a magazine or even a teacher you may somewhat fancy. My eyes did circles in my accountancy class whenever my teacher walked into the room. In fact, there were a handful of boys in the class who had their eyes on her instead of their credit ledgers. I'm sure it explains why I am hopeless with numbers to this day. I was far too busy focussing on other things.

For a large portion of males, lust develops at a point in their lives when there is no mutual relationship formed with the opposite sex. It begins as a selfish act with no reciprocation. There wasn't a physical relationship with my teacher except in my thoughts, which hung in mid-air, exclusively for me to know. There was nothing to ground me and pop the delusion of lust. The thought of 'coveting another human' never crossed my mind. I didn't even know what the word meant. Speaking of which, Jesus interestingly uses the same word for coveting in Matthew 5:28 that is found in the tenth commandment, 'You shall not covet your neighbour's wife' (Exodus 20:17 NIVUK). In other words, if you don't physically break the letter of the commandments but do so in your heart, you're guilty. God looks at the sinful heart; any heart desiring that which belongs to another is guilty. There's no grey area on this matter. The way I began to see women said a lot about what was forming in my heart.

In the lead-up to my wedding, I did the usual pre-marital counselling. Not because it was the norm or I felt compelled to but because it was a great way to talk openly about any reservations or things we might not have thought about. There were a lot of unknowns—things that never crossed our minds, especially as we were yet to live together. Every Wednesday I'd dash out of work and embark on the hour-long rush hour drive across the Irish border to my pastor's house. While my mind tried to settle the strain of the day, I tried to be present and engaged. I felt like these meetings were my only chance to settle any pre-marriage anxiety, like I was packing for a trip and crammed as much as I could into my bag, so I wouldn't forget anything. We soon learned everything from finance to communication, but, strangely, the chapter usually reserved for the end seemed to be skirted over. Our pastor briefly touched on the obvious things we both already knew. I was happy to spare the awkward sex talk, but deep down I felt that more would surface than our pre-marriage curriculum allowed. There had to be.

I wasn't searching for a technique or ten ways to plea-sure your spouse. I wanted to know why so many marriages in the past had been shattered because of sex, or lack thereof. I left the last meeting with more questions than answers.

I knew that sex was too big of a subject to share the same time slot with conflict resolution or children. So before we got married we both decided to work through a pre-marriage book that cuts through the nonsense about sex. In fact, it's all the book focuses on. Written by notorious former Mars Hill pastor Mark Driscoll, the pages are awash with everything you ever wanted to know about marriage and sex. Although his wife contributes to the book by balancing out some of his irreverence, it's still an unconventional Christian take that splits many readers across denominations. Despite what people think about the author's abrasive character, he still manages to make some sound points. I appreciated how the book bypassed the Cinderella fantasy and was not captive to political correctness or Christianese. I often struggled to find anything relat-able within contemporary Christian culture. It's not to say I vehemently dismissed everything, but few books are as unequivocally bold in a very conservative publishing landscape. I grew up having my mom shove James Dobson books down my throat. No offence to him personally, but his writing had zero relevance or profundity in my life. If anything, his books had more of a deluded effect on my mother, leaving the secondary distorted side effects of all things sexual to rub off on me. I'm convinced such overprotection and caution swung my proverbial pendulum towards fear. Sex was painted as mystical and esoteric, far too other-worldly for me to comprehend, shadowed in curiosity and guilt. It's no wonder the road map to lust was clearly marked for me.

A month out from our wedding, my wife and I decided that the best way to read this book was to each other as we drove down to church. We used to commute every Sunday from my wife's family home in the Northern Irish countryside to our church in Belfast. The drive took an hour or so, which made for entertaining, sometimes hostile, conversations, both there and back. The thing we loved most about one another was the absence of sugarcoating in our vocabulary—rawness and honesty allowed us to make up our minds by forcing us to challenge convention, as well as one another, openly. For instance, when I read a chapter about loving your wife—learning to see her as your standard of beauty, even when she gets fat—it jolted us, mainly me. I let the idea sink with me in the bucket seats of the Mini Cooper, navigating through the Celtic winter rain as it pelted the windscreen and drummed on the roof like a fast cadence.

Seeing my wife as my standard of beauty until eternity was such a confronting proposition. I certainly had never thought this way before. If I had heard this in my single years, I would've protested it as ludicrous. In reality, no one thinks about these perspectives and dynamics, and, in my experience, it's not taught in the broader church. Unless we advocate the idea of true beauty from an early age, men will always gravitate to an attitude of 'wanderlust,' lured by a raunchy centre-fold or a provocative website instead of the figure standing before you offering unconditional, authentic love. Your standard of beauty must move beyond looks to a place of true, intangible substance. Driscoll isn't regimental about passing attraction; I think he measures true beauty as the sum of the whole, not one lone value. Whatever your standard of beauty is, it should always be a constant despite any altering shapes and sizes, hair colours and lengths; it lives right in front of you in the present. It's right there if you see it.

The more I unpacked this idea, the more I discovered consistency in what the Bible says in directing our thoughts to our wives. God places value on the sanctity of relationships. The words of Jesus in Matthew on sexually coveting others is a clear warning, not a suggestion. We must direct these thoughts and deeds to our spouse. It is what standard of beauty is all about, not the influence of popular culture. Appreciating passing beauty isn't the problem, nor is it a sin. It's perfectly normal to be attracted to someone. We should celebrate beauty. But when we indulge, ruminate, seek to possess, or act on it, it's then that Jesus denotes it as adultery of the heart. *Attraction* is such a subjective and heavy-laden word that it can often mean many things to the eye of the beholder. It's important to recognise that attraction isn't to be confused with love or truth. It is far more fleeting and less grounded. I know I am guilty of such misappropriations.

Pope John Paul II articulates the value of attraction best in his book *Love and Responsibility* in a paragraph titled 'Love as Attraction':

> For when emotional reactions are spent—and they are naturally fleeting—the subject, whose whole attitude was based on such reaction, and not on the truth about the other person, is left as it were in a void, bereft of that good which he or she appeared to have found. This emptiness and the feeling of disappointment which goes with it often produce an emotional reaction in the opposite direction: a purely emotional love often becomes an equally emotional hatred for the same person. This is why in any attraction—and, indeed, here above all—the question of the truth about the person towards whom it is felt is so important. We must reckon with the tendency, produced by the whole dynamic of emotional life, for the subject to divert the question 'is it really so?' from the object of attraction to himself or herself, to his or her emotions. In these circumstances the subject does not enquire

whether the other person really possesses the values
visible to partial eyes, but mainly whether the
newborn feeling for that person is a true emotion . . .
People generally believe that love can be reduced
largely to a question of the genuineness of feelings.
Although it is impossible to deny this altogether, if
only because it follows from our analysis of
attraction, we must still insist, if we are concerned
with the quality of the attraction and the love
of which it is part, that the truth about the person
who is its object must play a part at least as
important as the truth of the sentiments. These two
truths, properly integrated, give to an attraction that
perfection which is one of the elements of
a genuinely good and genuinely 'cultivated' love.
Attraction goes very closely together with awareness
of values. A person of the other sex may cause
someone to experience a number of different values.
They all help to create the attraction, the dominant
emphasis in which, as we have said, is determined by
one particular value—that which has elicited the
strongest response. When we speak of truth in an
attraction (and by implication of truth in love) it is
essential to stress the attraction must never be limited
to partial values, to something which is inherent in
the person but is not the person as a whole.[1]

My battles with adultery of the heart, especially

pornography, were never kept a secret from my wife. She knew. Not every single sexual moment, but she was aware I had a problem. She knew this because I chose to tell her. We would often have frank discussions about it. Whenever I slipped up, I always promised to tell her, even if I knew full well I could keep it from her. I had grown up masking my behaviour, I was experienced enough to hide it from her if I really wanted to. I'm glad I told her though, because over time she became attune to my sudden shift in attitude—she was aware of signs that I'd slipped up before I could even strike up the courage to tell her first. This kind of candour in a relationship isn't easy for many. It takes two very understanding, committed souls.

A good friend of mine wasn't quite as receptive to my approach. He would never tell his wife when he had failed, not because of a lack of understanding on her behalf but more because he felt it would cause irreparable and unnecessary damage. In his own words, 'It wouldn't benefit anyone.' If he chose to be candid enough to open up, it would only be with a close male friend, someone like me. I got it. How is anyone supposed to explain how the feeling that they have, albeit a natural inclination, has become an unhealthy habit? I don't think there is a clear-cut approach. If confronted, honesty should always prevail, but I don't know of many men who'll tell their wives. I will say this though: when you lay something out, you see the stranglehold for what it is.

I empathise with the difficulty of opening up to the opposite sex for fear of intolerance or ignorance. It's often considered easier for men to relate to other men because they 'get it'; they've 'walked the walk' to some degree. The same applies to women who confide in women. Whether you call it a sisterhood or brotherhood, there's an assumed code of confidence. I don't necessarily agree with this sentiment; it begs a *laissez-faire* attitude that rests all too heavily on convenience of gender traits. It becomes a fraternity mentality, where what happens in the group stays in the group. This kind of thinking doesn't solve the feelings of the person you might be hurting on the other side. It certainly doesn't help educate them. Man or woman, we all need to understand this subject because it's vital to any relationship's trajectory and healing. The more our partners understand, the less chance there is that our addiction will become a dirty little secret.

If you're familiar with the actor Terry Crews, famous for being in films like *The Expendables* and *White Chicks*, you may also know that he's been quite vocal about his past battles with lust and pornography. He candidly chats about it in the video blogs he regularly posts on Facebook. He vocalises his struggle because he believes that silencing our weaknesses only makes them more powerful. When we choose to expose them, they lose power. The grip loosens. When I decided to be open with my wife, it allowed me to vocalise my weakness in the confines of our marriage—a safe and secure environment. The opposite would've added bricks to a wall, eventually dividing our familiarity, like resident Catholics and Protestants on Falls Road. It's why communication is key over mutual exclusivity. Sure, chatting with a bloke is often helpful, but this discussion shouldn't be confined only by gender. Understandably, in some cases, men fear to talk to their wives if they anticipate any hostile backlash. I too was sceptical. It took me a while to explain my actions to my wife. At times I felt like a teenager explaining why I arrived home at one minute past midnight. I had to gently ease into the subject until the association of taboo became acceptable. I recall one of the many conversations we had at our dinner table, where I took the opportunity to confess to my wife as she was taking her last bite of sweet potato fries. I never expected an easy reaction, and I never got it, but what always surprised me was how liberal she was with her forgiveness. Sure, there was anger and hurt, but never animosity. I recall that in one conversation, while over the last few bites left of our dinner, she bowled me her googly[2].

"So you look at other women more than your own wife?"...*record needle scratch*. I was stumped.

"Well, um, I wouldn't say more," I stammered. I was desperately searching for words to disarm the situation, regardless of how wrong I was. I had become a spin doctor, but she was having none of it. "Well, you're looking at their bodies and seem to prefer theirs over mine," she said, leaning forward a little. I knew telling her wasn't going to be a simple admission and acknowledgement. She was angry and resolute in her response to the situation. Despite her teacher-like demeanour, which at the time got my back up against the wall, I could see she was trying to help me to see it from her side. She needed to bring me out of the naive axiom of harmless fantasy to a realisation of a very damaging reality. And it was raw enough to convict me. Usually when I slipped up and looked at porn or looked lustfully at anyone other than my wife, I was so used to believing the salacious lie that male genetics had preconditioned me to be this visual creature who had no control—that I was a victim and couldn't possibly be responsible for hurting anyone when it's part of my physiological makeup. I had foolishly come to believe this, but thankfully my wife isn't as gullible. Although there are a lot of women who fall for the whole 'visual creatures' excuse, she knew better.

That night as I lay in bed, reflecting on my wife's words, I was aware of two things. First, I could not continue falling into the same trap of weak repentance, passing as a human error, only to stumble again. Second, although I always felt bad about lusting, it wasn't because I coveted another woman but because I believed the act of lust itself was sinful. My knowledge was limited, much like a child who knows to avoid touching a hot stove only because his mother said so, not because of a factual understanding that one might scold their hand if he so chooses to disobey. I respect parents who take the time to go into detail to explain to their children why something is wrong rather than just saying it's wrong and that's the way it is. The worst kind of admonishment is 'because the Bible tells me so'—a mantra I was nurtured on. Even though I was cognisant of my sins at an early age, I had no grounded knowledge of the *whys* behind my actions and *how* they might separate me from the ones I love or, even worse, hinder my relationship with God.

The more reality my wife shone forth into my life, the more illuminated my behaviour became. When you're single you con yourself into thinking that whatever you do is harmless because, well, you're single and it only involves you. There are no relational ramifications. Sure, you're hurting yourself, but, then again, your independence allows you to roll with the punches. I had imbibed this justification for years before settling into any stable relationships. I grew up training my mind to believe that my behaviour was okay until, eventually, it became so habitual that my brain naturally excused my unhealthy behaviour. So when my wife rightly convicted me, I wasn't entirely convinced of the sincerity of my repentance. My brain had become so habituated that it was too tortoise-like to counteract.

I found it increasingly difficult to register truth to address my issues immediately. A lot of my world was split between reality and online, so I never felt like my virtual existence was problematic in reality. I was almost convinced that my sins lived and stayed in the digital, hidden between the 1's and 0's. There were times when I would be aware of looking at a girl in the supermarket, yet I was utterly oblivious to the automatic click of my mouse button. This is how deluded I was. Here's the thing, though—through all the earnest chats with my wife, she never once mentioned the word *cheating*. It never surfaced. It didn't have to. Her words were heavy enough to sink in, dropping me onto a floor-bed of harsh reality, "So you prefer someone else's body to mine?" For the record, my wife is beautiful. Inside and out. Before we knew each other, I always thought she was the hottest girl in the room. Now that we're married, she still is. I'm under no illusion in the relationship who's clearly punching above their weight. *Moi.* When she pulled me up on my intentions to look at someone else, as ludicrous as it sounded, she was right to. I didn't feel cornered by her accusation but rather trapped inside my own paradox. Logic made it convincingly clear that my wife should be the only woman in the room to catch my eye. Wherever I go, my view should never deviate. The pleasure centre of my brain, on the other hand, still found it a challenge. What compelled me to flirt with fantasy when I had the best reality in front of me? It's one thing being physically monogamous, but it's another being mentally as well. There's always going to be someone prettier and younger, with better skin tones and complexion and a full head of hair.

This is the point Driscoll tries to make in his book: regardless of the women in the periphery, no matter someone else's age or beauty, no matter how low-cut the skirt, my wife should unanimously trump all. Always. The way she caught my eye before we even met should remain till death do us part. Again, the logic is abundantly clear. But in fleeting moments, it's not as simple. Beauty wilts, not only through time but with familiarity. The more one knows someone, the more dirt rises to the surface, floating around you like a Victorian bell-shaped crinoline. Opinions shift. Feelings dwindle.

Beauty isn't like the purlins between the rafters in a roof; it's not strong enough to prop a person alone or capable of holding its own. Maybe for an evening, but certainly not for eternity. If the Sistine Chapel had been left to hold its own over the years, it would have eventually weathered, peeled, and worn away, crumbling in on itself. As a protected trust, it has the good fortune of receiving preferential treatment to sustain its beauty.

You see my point. None of us will be preserved in this way. Looks might be the hook, but they're only temporary. There has to be something more that grounds us. Connects us. If my wife is to be my standard of beauty, then this standard must be built on a foundation stronger than looks alone. It has to be a far richer substance brewing within her, flowing outward. From the thoughts she thinks to the words she speaks, it all contributes to her beauty. Equally, there must be a mutual connection, respect, and willingness to see past the flaws. My wife would make the perfect 'brickie'; she's managed to Poly-Fil most of the cracks within me, plastering over and smoothing them out the only way she knows how.

Restoration is ever evolving as we learn about one other. It's the true test of time. Physical beauty isn't the only attractive characteristic. When I come home and connect and communicate with my wife and she really gets me, it far exceeds any physical attraction; she is someone who lets me be me. This is beauty. After all, it's why I fell in love with her in the first place. I told her this when I proposed: 'You're the only woman in the world who truly lets me be me.' I didn't want to marry her because she could rock a pair of skinny jeans. She was to me, but it wasn't what convinced me within the depths of my heart and soul. The ability to be yourself—your true self—around your partner is a hugely important aspect in any relationship: not to have to mould or adapt to someone's demands. Natural evolution as you grow together as a couple is expected, but not having to compromise your true self is fundamental. All other attributes are superfluous.

One of my good friends, who also happened to be a work colleague for years, thought very similarly to me, especially when it came to women. Fortunately, both of us are married now and our views have equally changed for the better. At the time though, we both struggled with the conventions of dating and all things girls. For example, when Greg or I would like a girl, someone who would catch our eye and cause our heart to pound heavily, the thought of her would go around in our brains like a tumble dryer on repeat, to the point where it became a kind of can't-get-you-out-of-my-head obsession. Round and round and round. It really was a never-ending cycle for us. I think it's one of the reasons we became such good friends: we kind of had this kindred spirit in the way we saw girls similarly. It was our *Seinfeld*esque view of the world. Just like Jerry and George, we'd often blow trivial things up to seem a lot larger than they really were.

One day while I was driving with Greg, he mentioned something which to this day has never left me. He had been seeing a psychologist at the time—I think for many reasons, but I didn't feel the need to ask. If anything, it was a place to verbalise all kinds of questions in a safe and qualified environment. He mentioned something resonant that his psychologist had said to him: a practical exercise he could put into action any time he saw a girl he liked. Something to helpfully stop any thought from turning into an obsession. I was intrigued, as I was equally guilty of this. He tapped his fingers on the steering wheels as if this revelation could break out into a musical at any minute.

"So anytime you see someone you like, someone who truly catches your eye, you should immediately go up and speak to them."

"Immediately?" I bounced back.

"Yeah, straight away."

"Why?" I asked. "What's the rush?"

"Well, you know how when we see a girl, you know, like the new intern at work?"

"Oh, I know her well, alright," I said, verbally nudging Greg in jest.

"Well, you don't actually, do you?" Greg was getting serious.

"Maybe not," I mumbled sheepishly.

Greg continued: "This is what I'm talking about. If you let this fantasy, or whatever you want to call it, play out in your head, it will always be a fantasy unless you go over and talk to her or whoever 'her' happens to be at the time."

"It's not as simple as it sounds," I defended.

"No, it's not, but it helps to disarm the fantasy."

His fingers stopped dancing between the ten and

two positions. He gripped the wheel in thought. He was silent for a few seconds as we sat idle at the traffic light. As the light turned green, it prompted a response that I thought was rather profound. I'm not sure if he was eloquently repeating what the shrink said or if they were his own words. Either way, it was genuine enough to strike a chord with me.

"Your thoughts will always remain a fantasy unless you physically bring them into reality."

"Deep," I whispered.

"You know what I mean, right?"

I did. Wise words, which I couldn't fault. Whether obsessing over a girl at work or mindlessly scrolling through an adult website, both instances are playing out some form of fantasy. We might not consciously be aware that they are, but inside our mind a story is fittingly written and woven into the fabric of a narrative that blurs the line between fact and fiction. It's knowing the difference between the two which allows us to interchange. Once we shed a light on reality, the pinhead of truth bursts the fantastical bubble. After a few friendly conversations, I soon discovered that the girls I once had imagined to be amazing were in fact not everything they had lived up to be in my mind. This realisation allowed me to dig deeper by removing myself from what I thought to be real and understanding that true intimacy and connection can never be experienced in the mind alone.

Years ago I heard a great saying from a Pastor about pornography: 'Once you see the woman on the other side of the screen as a father's daughter, someone's little girl, it's impossible to look at them the same way again.' They no longer remain an object of desire. They shift from a "thing" to somebody, someone who could be your own daughter one day.' The more I thought about what he said and the way I saw things, the more my perspective changed. When I look at another woman as an object of passion, it's antithetical to real love because it simply deprives her of possessing any positive human qualities. It causes me to act as if the other person were some sort of visual or emotional prostitute for my own gain. It really is selfish passion, regardless of your relationship status, because this selfishness distorts connection and acts against what is edifying and loving. My lusting didn't become a selfish thing when I was married and another life entered the picture. I was selfish already. But when you're married or dating, you betray the most intimate foundation: trust. Without trust, you have a rickety situation on your hands. You taint the sanctity of the bond you created spiritually, emotionally, and physically. Intimacy is where the hardest blow is dealt. As an addict it becomes difficult to give all of yourself when you've lost a good part of you to your addiction. Equally, the victim loses a space of safety and vulnerability. While trust can definitely be rebuilt, it's important not to get it confused with forgiveness. Trust takes time, whereas forgiveness is about the right time. One is earned, the other is a choice.

Lust wants to take. It won't stop when it has had enough; it'll only take more because it will never be satisfied. Lust isn't a slave, but a master. It demands your all, making it impossible to live out and seek the Lord's will in your heart. There isn't room for two masters.

Love does the reverse. It puts the other person first —always. When we cherish those around us as brothers and sisters in Christ, all part of a bigger spiritual family, we won't put ourselves in situations where we're tempted to indulge ourselves and dehumanise women. And the longer we resist a particular temptation, the less power it will exercise over our lives.

I realised that whenever I lust after another woman, I'm taking a transitory part of that person. I have no inclination as to who this person is or what makes her unique. I understand only a small part of her. There is no real substance as to who she really is. My interest is only a physiological gratification, no different from seeing a flashy product advertised. When I lust after another woman, I replace my wife with the woman I objectify, not because she is better looking but because I allow myself to play host to a condition which has gorged on me for years. The more I see, the more I become plagued, and the more it sparks a response in me.

I realised that my thoughts and desires, whether while looking at a glossy centrefold or the next-door neighbour sunbathing, weren't because of a physical preference over my wife. I wasn't on some search for an earthly Aphrodite but for something far deeper. The more I excavated, the more my senses were heightened and aroused and the more my brain learned to attribute a stimulated response with the particular feeling or situation.

In psychology, they call this a trigger response. It helped me see through the malaise, revealing that what I was sexually addicted to had nothing to do with the image I lusted after in the first place. The response might have always been the same, but how I repeatedly got there was less relevant. I suppose it's why I never saw myself as cheating: I never placed any importance on the trigger. Once I identified all my reasons for acting out on lust, it was easier for me to find ways to work on myself and combat it the next time I was tempted. Understanding this helped me become aware of my sense of control, making it easier for my wife and I to work through my situation and make progress. I generally know when my triggers will hit. Not always, but if I am in a specific situation or feeling a particular emotion at a certain time, I'm aware that I may succumb to acting out, often without much thought.

When my wife convicted me at the table about my wandering motives, it wasn't the slap on the wrist that stirred my heavy emotions but a hole within that I somehow was trying to fill. Whether it was job satisfaction or something that I had been wrestling with from childhood, it was only when I identified what was holding me captive that freedom could be attained. Only then would the light lead to a place where true beauty shines: my standard of beauty.

Beauty

I wasn't in a 'serious' relationship until I was in university. And even then it wasn't serious. You could say I was a late bloomer to the notion of having consideration for others. Throughout my high school years, I had been a law unto myself, which meant my brain was ripe for being conditioned by any of my selfish desires. The day my school friends handed me a racy VHS was the beginning of my association with sex, women, and my own visceral and physiological gratification. There wasn't any exchange of pleasantries with or permission from any of the women behind the analogue display. To me, this was nothing more than a rite of passage to growing up. I certainly had no remorse over cheating or dehumanising, especially not in any visceral sense. When Jesus spoke about lust, it never seemed to apply to me. It felt so otherworldly and grown-up, as if it applied only to men in power suits sneaking off with impressionable secretaries. But I no longer believe that this topic comes in shades of grey, and neither should you. Here's why. First, any promiscuous image used to proposition men—be it a centrefold, chat room, or sexually explicit clip—has a real person behind it selling themselves for the gratification of others. They know full well what they have to do to elicit the desired effect. Second, for some reason, we live in a world where the word online softens the consequence. I didn't pirate, I just downloaded. I didn't defame, I just tweeted. I didn't hack, I was just looking. The reality is that your husband or boyfriend is committing fraud in a domain that should be exclusively yours.

6

ARE YOU MISSING WHAT'S RIGHT IN FRONT OF YOU?

IT WAS A SWELTERING HOT DAY IN DECEMBER, AND I had a craving for seafood. I was on holiday in South Africa and was meeting my friend Justin for lunch. The whole way there all I could think about was a tray of oysters on a bed of ice with a slice of lemon and a splash of Tabasco, and washing it down with a cold, Jozi beer. I arrived at a packed restaurant with patrons already retreating indoors, escaping the dense heat for the air-conditioning. Only a few tables were left outside under the cool liquid haze of the high-pressure water misters. I felt like a bottle in a beer commercial, continually being spritzed to appear crisp and refreshing. As I stretched out to absorb the coolness, I spotted a tall, attractive, blonde waitress making her way to our table. I quickly aligned my body, clumsily knocking my knee against the table, trying desperately not to

wince from the pain. She laid out our Afro-Mediter-
ranean feast and, with a disarming charm, smiled and
told us to enjoy our meals. As she sauntered off, I
impatiently grabbed a fork and dislodged the oyster,
placing it to my lips, loudly sucking it as hard as I
could. Justin laughed as I reached for another.

"How have you been?" He sank back in his chair.
Justin and I are firm believers in brevity, with a disdain
for small talk. We cut straight to it.

"Is it even possible to look at women without lust?"
I mused. I saw the humour in the clichéd aphrodisiac
that I was drowning in Tabasco. "How do you distinguish?" I continued.

"Theology of beauty, man," he said, still struggling
with his pre-shucked oyster.

"What do you mean?"

For a brief moment, he placed the shell on his side
plate to return to it later. "I'm fulfilled." His answer
was as calm as the reply.

"Fulfilled, like sexually?" I pressed.

"Yes, but it's so much more." He leaned forward
and began to unpack his theory. "I'm fulfilled in what I
have. You have to be. It's not about wanting something
else, it's about looking at what you do have."

"Go on," I egged. We always said this when we
wanted the other person to unpack a point of view
further.

"When you covet, you do not appreciate what you

do have. And what you do have, Steve, is a gift. When you covet, you believe you deserve something. When you choose to lust after another woman, not only do you believe you deserve her, to some degree, but you're equally implying you deserve your wife, the woman you've already married. Do you see what I mean?"

I half-heartedly nodded, still trying to digest the words (and a slice of olive loaf).

"You see, the problem isn't with all the women you're lusting after," he continued. "It's with the one woman you already have in your life, which, clearly, you think you've deserved." He scratched his stubble as if he was figuring how he could conclude his thoughts on the size of a Post-it note.

"When you realise your wife is a gift and not rightfully yours, then you understand true fulfilment." He paused, took a sip of his beer, and picked up his lone oyster again. "And when you realise this, then you understand the theology of beauty: a woman walking past you who catches your eye is beautiful, but when your gaze is not lustful, you begin to see them as they truly are." He eventually sucked the oyster down and, with a subdued grin, continued, "This is not foolproof. It's just not taught."

"What do you mean?" I finally interjected.

"This part of thinking is not taught in our daily theology. We are not taught to see our partners as a gift —especially not men—and to treat them as such. We see women as something to be owned. Whether in our minds or through physical control."

I couldn't fault what he said. I'd seen men get quite territorial, like deer during rutting season. 'I realise I struggle to see women as only beautiful and nothing more' I said.

"Yeah, sure, and so did I," he continued, "but think of it as 'pre' versus 'post.'" "You're worried about the post effect, when surely the prior is where you should start."

"Metaphorically, at home," I quipped.

"Yes! Start with the girl in front of you," he suggested. "She can walk out of your world tomorrow. You have no certainty, nor do you have control."

"She's a gift," I concluded.

"She's a gift," he reciprocated. "And a gift that needs to be cherished. You see, once you truly realise what you have . . ." He momentarily paused, then leaned in. "Steve, Mel's beautiful and more than you could've imagined, right? Think about the moment you knew she was the one."

I was doing precisely that and feeling slightly ashamed.

"Think of losing what you have. You don't own her; she's not yours. And when you realise God has put this woman in your life, then you realise what true fulfilment is."

I quickly jumped in: "Then why do so many guys cheat? Is it because they're unfulfilled?"

Before he could respond, he signalled for the waitress, then picked up his glass and tilted it, holding up two fingers to motion for more drinks. She nodded and wandered back inside.

"I think there's many reasons, irrespective of whose fault it is. All I can say is this, when it comes to guys looking elsewhere, it's because they're not fulfilled."

"I noticed you didn't say, 'unfulfilled.'"

"Yeah exactly, sometimes there are relationships that suffer from a lack of fulfilment, but it doesn't always mean a person is unfulfilled with their partner. I think there's unrealised truth in overlooking what you already have. That's why so many people who are unhappy in a relationship always tend to look elsewhere. In this instance, short-sightedness is encouraged instead of squinting at silhouettes in the distance. They're not living in the now."

I was slowly circling the circumference of my glass, taking in what he had said and refocusing on my relationship.

"So with me, right, even though I lust, it doesn't mean I have an unfulfilling marriage or relationship."

"Exactly!" He slammed the table with the palm of his hand, causing the cutlery to clink and the couple next to us to look over. His inflection subdued.

"Your lack of fulfilment is causing you to lust, but it's because you don't realise what you have in the first place. You're looking at it all wrong. You're trying to diagnose the issue of lust and not the issue of fulfilment."

We returned to our meal and ate mostly in silence. I realised I was wanting to find some kind of magic bullet, a cause and effect that would allow me to get to the root of my lust so I could nip it in the bud. I mulled over the conversation, and although there was a lot of truth to what he said, I also believed his solution was not clear-cut. Apart from the psychological side of reward experienced by the pleasure centre in our brain, a lot of our lustful actions are the result of a lack of fulfilment—a sign that something is clearly missing in our lives. A part of it is spiritual, and this is true of anyone, no matter your faith. Trials and tribulations will seem impossible when there's an absolute absence of spiritual edification. As I mentioned in an earlier chapter, the whole notion of cloaking ourselves in spiritual armour, whether it sounds fantastical to you or not, has some practical application for me. It's a conscious reminder of how, every day, I am susceptible to things all around me. If my eyes are not focused on the things above, then I'm likely to be distracted by whatever crosses my path or pops up on my screen late at night.

A lack of fulfilment can also be evident in our friendships, in our marriages, or amongst those with whom we work. It's less about not getting what you think you need (although sometimes this is true), and more about being unaware of what you might already have. It was certainly true in my own life. I either felt that something was amiss, or I was told by a psychologist something was missing in my life. After a few oysters and a heart-to-heart, I realised that the fundamental problem was how I framed the question in the first place. The right question to ask was: What in my life have I not been thankful for?

Giving thanks can initiate a major turning point in one's life. It's why I love the tradition celebrated every year amongst Americans and Canadians. Thanksgiving is about a time of reflection and being grateful for the proverbial harvest in our lives. I have a lot of American friends who make an even bigger deal of this occasion than Christmas. Even though I don't celebrate the former, I've observed how my friends use this day to stop everything and connect with those they love most. I think the whole world could use a day where we slow down and give thanks for the things, experiences, friends, and family we have. It's so easy to fall into a space where we worry about whether we'll have a job tomorrow or be able to get a mortgage for the house we saw on Saturday. Do we ever instead just give thanks for what we already have?

I know that it's easy for me to focus on what I don't have, what I haven't accomplished, what I've missed out on, or the validation I'm still seeking. I measure my worth by casting my eyes outwards. Very rarely do I stop to look at what's right in front of me; instead, I'm either living in the past or jumping ahead to the future. It takes a lot of hard work for me just to be present and appreciative in the moment. This sense of always looking forward only fuels fear. It's a battle for me every day, especially with lust. As long as my eyes are open, they are susceptible—vulnerable to all the images of what the world is telling me I should strive towards, what I must have, and how my existence isn't complete until I have the thing that I am looking at. Every day I have a choice to remind myself to stop chasing the must-haves; I already have an abundance right in front of me.

Gratitude

I've often heard the phrase, 'Life is a verb, not a noun.' Life isn't static. It cannot be contained or manipulated. It evolves and constantly moves forward. And as long as it's in motion we need to experience it by living in the now. If we're too busy overthinking life and getting lost in thoughts of the past or the future, we aren't really living. We're simply existing, which isn't what we're designed for. Living life can be experienced only through letting go. Only then are we free from debilitating lies about the past or future. Richard Branson once said, 'We're called human beings, not human doings.' No matter what we do, no matter how much we try, if we don't allow ourselves to 'be,' we won't ever be fulfilled. Allowing ourselves to be means allowing ourselves to love what's in front of us and to be loved back. When I started to do this, I naturally stopped looking at what I thought was best for me and instead began to experience the best of me.

7

WELCOME TO RAT PARK

WHEN YOU HEAR THE WORD *ADDICT*, WHAT SPRINGS TO mind? Is it the same generic imagery as mine, borrowed from shows like *The Wire* and *NYPD Blue*? The setting's always seedy—a cascade of green sepia tones bleeding across the backdrop of an abandoned apartment in some derelict, downtown neighbourhood. Inside, a skinny white dude is slumped over a mattress just before the cops burst through the doors and Detective Sipowicz saunters in reading the Riot Act while mopping his sweaty forehead with his handkerchief. The victims appear malnourished and sick. Among the clutter and unnecessary hoarding, you can hear a baby screaming somewhere in the distance (there's always a baby screaming).

This notion of an addict smacks of the usual tropes, but it denotes association. Over the years, I've realised it's not all fictional. These preconceived ideas would slowly change in parallel with my own life. The more I wrestled with my struggles, the more I realised that addiction isn't as predictable as Hollywood paints it. It often masquerades in many forms that are not always keen to the eye.

Unwanted sexual addiction isn't specifically one thing. It's incredibly difficult to label because it constitutes many moving parts that intertwine at different junctures. Someone can be a compulsive philanderer, having an insatiable sexual appetite. Others might display components deemed a little more abstract— namely, serial dating, sadistic or masochistic behaviour, exhibitionism/voyeurism, idolatry, obsessive infatuation, infidelity, prostitution, and, of course, porn. It boils down to lust of the heart, but even *lust* is an abstract word. I spent ages pontificating the definition of my own sexual plight, but obsessing over the right classification didn't make it any more definitive. It was and is an addiction of the sexual kind. Such a recognition in itself is the beginning, and it's enough to begin a freeing journey.

Whatever you choose to call your own sexual struggle, it is an *idée fixe* atypical to other addictions. Unlike chemical addictions, it mostly manifests in secret—deeply rooted below the skin where scars are rarely visible. Everything is disguised behind the notion of the 'natural urge.' It's not an immediate death either, but a slow emotional and spiritual one, killing your soul over time. As strange and disturbing as it sounds, I'm often jealous of other addictions because it doesn't take long before you can witness a cry for help.

When I have seen and experienced the signs of other addictions, there's always been one common denominator: they often prompt a visual or behavioural reaction. It's why sexual addiction is often referred to as a process addiction; it's unlike other addictions where you physically use a substance. It's also less visual than others. What I mean by this is an alcoholic can only cover up for so long before the dependency becomes public knowledge: a deteriorating health, yellowing of the eyes and skin, broken capillaries, brittle hair and fingernails, and a marked decrease in attention to personal hygiene, including the noticeable, lingering odour of 'drink' on the breath.

The other thing worth noting is that sex, as a natural part of our life, can shape part of our identity, alter our moods, and impact us psychologically and spiritually. It's also harder to suppress that which is inherently ingrained in us. A confusing push-and-pull battle ensues in our minds instead, making relapse unavoidable. Rather than complete abstinence, a different approach is required. You must observe certain behaviours and commit to retraining impulses often understood to be normal.

A huge part of my own battle had to do with my limited knowledge of the psychology behind my own behavioural response. It's not as simple as total sobriety. As hard as I tried to shake my addiction, it was impossible for me to suddenly change the reward patterns that my brain had developed over time. It would be like changing the familiar frequency of the bell that triggered Pavlov's dog to salivate. New tricks take time and I'm not getting any younger. I claim no psychology or neuroscience training, but I firmly believe that part of the recovery process involves understanding why your mind and body react the way they do. Until I understood the *why*, I did not have clarity about the true scale of my problem. And you change the problem only by changing the mind.

It's also important to point out that knowing the science won't completely save you either. If anything, it'll help you understand yourself better and move past the defeatist response of blaming lust on a natural biological urge. Claiming natural inclination as an excuse would hold true if we didn't embody the ability of reason. But we're humans, not animals. In all honesty, my excuse was that I chose not to fight unwanted and unnatural desires when I should have. Admittedly, even if I challenged my vice head-to-head, I had no idea what I was truly up against. So how could I expect to have any control at all? Had I any free will? The only reason that seemed reasonable was my acceptance of unconscious and repeated lusting without having any memory as to how I got there in the first place. As soon as a flicker went off in my brain, I endured the notion that I was too far gone to be stopped, and time literally jumped forward.

So I started to do my own research, reading what I could to help me get a better position on top of this unruly beast. I read countless books and online articles on addiction, and what helped me most was understanding how our brains, filled with certain chemicals, function and respond. I'm sure you've heard of neurotransmitters like serotonin and dopamine. Dopamine is a chemical in our brain released whenever we feel a sense of pleasure, and it plays a huge role in controlling our motivations and reward pathways. Think about the state of ecstasy your body and mind feel when you eat a slab of your favourite chocolate—a sudden rush of sugary pleasure to the brain. It's the inner workings of dopamine.

With something like lust, this whole process feels haphazard because, of course, our brain is flooded with dopamine. It's like the movie *The Perfect Storm*, where the boat is repeatedly slammed and engulfed by waves of water. It's how it feels upstairs in our brain. And like any addiction, when you try to deny it, your body screams out to be drowned in the same flurry of giddiness. There were days when I wouldn't have a sexual thought, then suddenly my body would crave a visual stimulus. The problem was, as I continued to feed my desires and let them fester, they grew beyond my capability of commanding any control over my actions. And the more my body and mind became accustomed to this way of thinking, the more it felt like a natural habit. I would often find myself at the worst moments of my addiction objectifying anything and anyone. I just needed something visual because I could feel my body wanting.

Sometimes it would happen in unexpected places, the worst being in church, especially as a pubescent boy. It was almost impossible for a fifty-minute sermon to hold my attention without my eyes wandering and my thoughts running rampant. It's a challenge for any teenager to hold his concentration for an extended amount of time. My mind was like a vacuum, sucking up anything in its way, anything I could objectify. It didn't matter how, with who or what. I'd find a way to get my high: in church, walking past female fitness magazines on a shelf, seeing a provocative billboard, watching the girls' field hockey team training after school, or subtly peeking at the lingerie in the women's section while out shopping with my mom. I could go on. I'm certainly not alone in this. Most guys would agree, having experienced similar scenarios. It's how my hunger began.

The human condition is a funny thing. It always tries to push past the limit, curious to see how far it can go. It's like when I first came across a food waste disposal in the sink of a house I was renting. I would scrape off my leftovers, flick the switch, and joyously hear the gnashing of the metal blades as the waste was sucked down and disappeared into the dark depths below. It felt liberating. Every item of food had its own unique torturous sound. Experimenting was so addictive until, of course, it eventually backed up.

We're curious creatures at heart, and we all have a morbid fascination with pushing the boundary. The problem is that curiosity at such a young age, unchecked, can be problematic—it's why we have parents and rules. Nobody questions the rule of not touching a hot plate on an oven. It's universally obvious. The effects are immediate and painful. But looking at a lingerie catalogue that slipped out of a magazine doesn't sound like such a big deal. To most people it sounds mild, even lame by today's standards. I didn't have internet while growing up or any access to hardcore pornographic magazines, certainly not the way kids are exposed to it today. The beginning of my curiosity was gradual and seemingly mild. It wouldn't have caught anyone else's attention, let alone mine. I was oblivious to the years of internal torment about to follow. From a young age, most children are taught that drugs are dangerous and can do permanent harm despite fleeting satisfaction. It might not be enough to deter everyone, but it certainly precludes a lot of people from entertaining the very thought. In my experience, the dangers of sexual addiction aren't taught to young people. It was non-existent in my school days. I'm not sure what it's like now, but I can't imagine that it's any better. There's sex ed, sure, but from my recollection it was more an anatomical discussion than life guidance.

If you ever attended church, you've probably heard about sex narrated in historical accounts before most kids did, which is not to say you were any wiser. People with unpronounceable names belonging to tribes, philandering, committing debauchery, and making God considerably angry—these accounts felt far-fetched and intangible. What is lust of the flesh anyway? It sounded like something out of a zombie movie—a concept impossible for me to grasp at such a young age. It was up there in the Bible with killing and stealing: something I shouldn't do if I didn't want to disappoint God. I was left with more questions than answers. Sex was a concept; not a possibility. No one ever called me into a room and taught me about the signs and dangers of objectifying women. I could pinpoint Golgotha on a map to my Sunday School teacher far easier than I could identify lustful thoughts.

I get that it's not the easiest topic to kick about at Sunday school. You can't exactly broach the subject of lust without giving a visual example first. Sunday school teachers aren't going to hold up a *Playboy* centrefold to a bunch of ten-year-olds, now, are they? Attention-grabbing as it would be, it would spark an outcry. Here's an absurd comparison: even in the current climate over mass shootings in America, the National Rifle Association is welcomed in many classrooms to teach gun safety to six year olds. In fact, many of them are even allowed to hold a semiautomatic. Whichever side of the political fence on which you may sit, the absurdity that it exists should make a discussion on sexual addiction a breeze to talk through. Yet I wonder how many school teachers hold up a provocative advert and ask their class to talk about what's wrong with the picture. Sex is a subject that should be demystified and explained, whether in schools or at home. How it's done is immaterial, as long as it's done. If we're going to teach young boys before they become men that it's not okay to objectify women, the classroom might be a good place to start shaping impressionable minds.

I'm a sucker for factual programs. One thing I love to do is watch British documentaries. I think they have the whole investigative reporter style and nuances down pat. Perhaps their accent makes anything sound slightly more dramatic and earnest. One particular program that caught my eye was a documentary on Channel 4 called *Porn on the Brain*. It investigates how teenagers' pornography habits have changed and the effects that today's access has on their brains. It's hosted by an ex-editor of a lads' mag—the same lads' mag I used to sell advertising space for when I was gaining some overseas experience at the largest publishing company in Britain.

What fascinated me most about the documentary were the revealing insights, particularly how our current pornography behaviours have seemingly gotten worse as we've adapted to the internet age and a shift towards technology. Most people acknowledge this fact as glaringly obvious. However, I doubt they would be able to tell to what degree it affects the brain or how bad it's gotten for most people. My only criticism is that while the presenter communicates the behavioural side effects of pornography in today's society, he also insists how harmless it was twenty years ago, as if porn back then somehow had its act together. He glosses over the real issue of sexual addiction, which isn't prejudiced to time.

A sixty-minute documentary is never going to cover sexual addiction in its entirety, but *Porn on the Brain* did manage to show the raw grip that pornography has on a young adult in real time. In it the presenter follows a young man from London like an eager new dog behind its owner. Every minute is captured, hoping to catch the apparent problem the subject clearly struggles to shake. I had never seen such a candid account about this subject, I was even more impressed with how the young man didn't appear ashamed to bare it all while the cameras rolled. I think it took a lot of guts to do so. I have huge respect for him. What struck me most was how quickly he admitted his lack of control, but with his life playing out on camera in the midst of his struggles, it would have been impossible to hide anything.

I remember a scene of him driving down a suburban road and stopping at a traffic light. He was suddenly less chatty than usual. Only the hum of the idle engine could be heard. He was fixed on something or someone. The camera tracked his eyes as they followed two girls crossing the street in front of him. They were in mid-conversation, oblivious to the fact that they unflinchingly caught his attention and the cameras. All of a sudden he was fidgety and preoccupied in thought. He wore a sorry, glazed look. Noticing a shift in mood, the presenter prodded for a reaction, snapping him from a state of trance. He had the look of a man possessed. As the traffic light changed, he snapped out of his trance into the present and without restraint talked through what was going on in his mind. Somehow the two pedestrians triggered something in him. There was no nudity or sexual provocation. Yet when asked why they caught his gaze, he replied, "It's the way they walked." A walk. Something so vague and nondescript. It became evident that the walk wasn't a suggestive act but a trigger that unlocked a treasure chest of imagery in his brain. The triggers eventually became so bad that he had to pull over at the nearest pub and relieve his itch in the toilets. Thankfully, the cameraman stayed behind.

I'm not entirely sure it was staged; it didn't appear to be. It felt raw and unnerving. His honest account of affliction wasn't any worse or unfamiliar than watching a drug addict in relapse fighting the urge of 'shooting up.' It's clear that his mind had been completely reprogrammed by sexual compulsion—so much so that it trumped any intimate relationship he could possibly muster. He was quite vocal about the lack of enjoyment he experienced with physical sex. By his own admission he didn't miss the act, as it was never the same high for him. Interestingly, he never opened up about intimacy, or the lack thereof.

For the sake of science he eventually conceded to conduct an MRI scan live on air. The results were astonishing. As soon as he was shown erotic images on the screen, his brain lit up like a digital billboard in Times Square. What really surprised me was when the doctor compared his neural activity to a drug addict's. It became evident that he was as much of a compulsive user as someone trapped by heroine. His patterns and responses showed little difference from a hard-core drug user's; both addictions have a physiological craving and a chemical reaction. One requires entry through the blood to the brain, the other through the eyes to the brain. The only difference with something like porn is that it's unregulated, so most people can stumble across it quite easily. Its digital ubiquity makes it impossible to ignore without going to the extreme measure of becoming a Luddite. I might not completely relate to the young guy in the Channel 4 documentary, but I understand what it's like to have something pulling at you every hour of the day until it gets its own way. The documentary left me feeling sad for him because of the enormity of his burden. His young life seemed void of any interests, passions, or hobbies. When he looked into the camera his eyes appeared like black windows that peered into a vast, dark space. It seemed as though he didn't do anything else in his life apart from porn and university—in that order.

There's another side to the chemical and biological aspects of addiction. In the 1970s, research was conducted where two bottles filled with water were placed on either side of a metal rat cage. The only difference between them was that one was drugged with heroin. Expectedly, the rat would get addicted to the drugged water, avoid the clean water, and eventually die. The results clearly proved that the chemical pull of addiction is uncontrollable.

Unknown to most, a scientist in the same era by the name of Bruce Alexander was conducting similar experiments on rats. He believed that the confining, insular cage played an influential part in compulsive, unwanted habits. So he jazzed up the space like some renovation reality series. He went all out on the budget and created a rat park, making it an enjoyable experience: a playground filled with other rats and all the food they could ever want, while still having free access to drugs. But the rats avoided becoming addicted altogether. He didn't stop the experiment there either. He removed the rats from the park and temporarily housed them in an empty cage, much like the original experiment, force-feeding them drugs for fifty-seven days until they were solely addicted. He then returned them to the rat park and waited. The results were remarkable. Astonishingly, the rats had the innate capability to eventually wean their drug use over time, reversing the initial addiction. Alexander's research wasn't out to disprove chemical dependency as a fallacy, but rather to highlight the influential role of other peripheral factors.

I understand how isolation exacerbated my addiction. I wasn't confined to a cage, but the reality of changing countries meant that I felt further away from familiarity and comfort. Nature was often the welcomed friend I would turn to. I loved getting outdoors as much as possible, but sometimes it wasn't an option. Either the weather revolted or the prospect of weekday micro-adventures seemed less alluring on a school night. Over time, my online fascination increased with the introduction of social media. Like most, I'd pore over Instagram feeds, hunched and transfixed on the myriad career outdoor adventurists.

Admittedly, the odd allure of vicariously living through their high-on-life filtered thumbnails seemed far more interesting than the humdrum of my own life. This avoidance only left me feeling dissatisfied with the push and pull of my endless struggle. I would often find guys in my own circles of friends, adventurous types, who always seemed to be busying themselves with life. They could somehow make going to the newsagent to pick up milk look like an adventure. They always appeared to have something going on in life, either with entrepreneurial projects or travel expeditions, training for some big endurance event, or communing in various group activities—these were the same guys who for some reason never seemed to battle with lust. They weren't immune by any measure. They're still blokes with hormones. They have eyes and guy bits, but for them they never dwelled. They never allowed unwanted thoughts or behaviour to pull them away for hours the way it did with me. Sure, they might stumble across something provocative, or a beautiful woman might catch their eye somewhere, but they never seemed to let it grab them in such a way that it consumed their whole life. By no means are they immune, they are, however, free from its overbearing foothold. These types of characters are a small percentage; a percentage I can only speculate. I knew only a few growing up. What I admire most and draw inspiration from is how they choose to live life in front of a GoPro, not staring behind a screen in a darkened bedroom.

The hardest part of addiction is not knowing when it's coming. There's no warning. It doesn't drop an email expecting you to accept a calendar invite to schedule in your 'fix.' I might not have known how, but I had a pretty good idea that my hunger would be fed soon after experiencing certain triggers. My most vulnerable time is downtime or when I'm mentally drained. When I'm idle, temptation seems to heighten. I've now put buffers in place, but when I had all the time to myself, I was at my most vulnerable. Like any addiction, it robbed me of however much time it needed to take until left satisfied.

Living alone didn't help. Throughout my twenties I rented apartments for one. I was done with house sharing. I dreaded the idea of waking up every morning having to juggle different personalities and temperaments. Talking was not something I looked forward to after a long day at work. As an introvert, I found being on my own far more appealing because it provided me with a safe space to retreat to when my social gauge would overheat. An emergency lever I knew I could pull at any time. It was always calming to come back to a place of stillness. It re-energised me. I cherished and feared it. Although I often felt pure joy, I could also feel the pull of a dark presence, lurking in the wings, waiting for its stage entry. I'd feel the soft tap on my shoulder, and the hours would eventually propel to a blur. It's how it always happened. On the outside it might have appeared that I lived alone, but I was living with something far more demanding of my time than I was prepared to handle. If I were to calculate the amount of hours I lost throughout the course of my life to unwanted sexual behaviour, it would sorely add up to four years—possibly even more. When I think of what I could've achieved with all that lost time—quantifiable hours in which I had no responsibilities to marriage or kids—it leaves me heavy with regret to this day.

If you're familiar with Dr. Jordan B Peterson, the controversial celebrity pop psychologist, you might also have also stumbled across the lectures he candidly posted on YouTube. In one particular post, he lectures to his students about the value of time: how placing a quantifiable figure on every hour spent as a commodity will change how constructively you spend it. In other words, if time is valuable, then how much do we really value it? Realistically, how much would your time be worth? Fifty dollars an hour? One hundred? More? You might assume more, but the only way to increase value is if you have spent your time well. How are you growing your worth, net or otherwise? How are you upping your levels of knowledge, skill, relationships, spirituality, health? You could be forty and still of low value. Then, of course, there's the financial cost of the time you've already wasted, which it pains me to think about how much I've lost. I can rebuild my wealth, but I cannot regain time.

I would liken this loss to the feeling of arriving home from a well-needed holiday only to walk through the doors to find your place ransacked. As you move through each room of your house carrying out a mental roll call on all of your prized possessions, you begin to tally all the things you've lost—some with profound personal significance and full of memories, others expensive in taste, albeit fleeting in entertainment. The more you search through the chaos and disorder, the more emotions you feel. Initially there's a sense of panic, followed by confusion, anger, and finally despair.

These are some of the things I felt immediately after our family's home was broken into. I was still living at home, and my parents had gone away for the week and left me in charge. Upon returning home late from work one night, I discovered that we had been robbed. Despite the initial material loss, the frustration of police reports, and the emotional jolt to my system, it was only when weeks had passed that I soon discovered greater emotional larceny. It left a mark and changed me forever. For years after the break-in I locked everything a million times to the point of being borderline OCD. Whether I locked a suitcase for a flight or my car parked outside a supermarket a hundred times, it took a lot to convince me. I had gone from carefree to being fearful. Expecting the worst, I would do everything I could to prevent anything like this from ever happening again.

It's the same with sexual addiction. When we look beyond our initial loss and see the frays and cracks formed within our character, leaving nothing but permanent scars, only then do we realise what's left. Understandably, we do everything in our power to safeguard our domain from any further damage. I'm now more aware of my time and how I should use it. I don't want to lose a second. Had I been more constructive, I could've done so much more with all the minutes, hours, and days lost. I could've worked on being a better husband to my wife. I could've taken up a hobby, studied further, read more, written way more, perhaps even produced something (like this book). Instead of focusing on the 'could haves, would haves, should haves' amongst the loss of time, I became forever determined to rebuild and treasure every second I have. When we start to recognise what we have been robbed of, the process of renewal truly starts to bear fruit.

Yet, even as I write this, every day is still a battle for me. Like any person who's lost a sense of control in their life, I guess, that's the challenge I face. I don't live in a bubble; temptation comes from many angles. As long as my eyes are open, my mind's susceptible. But that doesn't mean I'm hopeless. I initially thought I had to be clean to write this book, to be perfect; otherwise, who would want to read it? I'm not perfect, but I now have enough insight to take on the day. Although experience affords me this, it doesn't automatically guarantee a change. It's why going into every detail of my sexual antics isn't going to educate you as much as it would provoke you. My hope is to illuminate a way to help you understand the man you are (or for that matter the man in your life) and to know you're not alone. Addiction isn't an easy fix; recovery can be a long, hard road, and sometimes you aren't aware you need help. Even if you're successful in removing the addictive habits—whether it's alcohol, drugs, or sex—there's still a vacancy needing to be filled, and it's our natural human desire to want to replace an existing absence. Instead of plastering over the cracks with something fleeting, recovery requires an eternally fulfilling way.

This 'hole' that everyone needs to fill is often a spiritual void. It's not something we can physically find, yet we all have a suspicion that it's somewhere inside of us, and it's empty. This void is often echoed in the memoirs of rock stars, with their journey of substance abuse to sobriety involving a spiritual quest of some kind. Not all of them have a Damascus Road, 'come to Jesus' moment. Some have stumbled on Buddhism, meditation, or twisting body parts into awkward positions. Regardless of their path, there's a spiritual undertone, an inward exploration that's required. And once the foundation has been identified, it's then a case of rebuilding a structure that will eventually close the process of recovery. The American bassist from the band Megadeth, David Ellefson, sums up his recovery in his biography *My Life with Deth*:

> Once you remove the drugs and alcohol, there's a spiritual void, and that's what gets filled up through God and the process eventually led me to finding faith. I just couldn't stop, and when I stopped on my own I couldn't stay stopped on my own. I needed faith to make it work . . . We all need to be transformed in order to defeat our addictions. We learn new disciplines to replace old ones. It takes work: it's not enough to simply sit at home and say, "Isn't this great? I'm saved! I'm good to go." No. We need prayer and instruction and fellowship. We need all of those things, because they form the process of recovery.[1]

For me, the process of discipline, prayer, communion, and teaching is what continues to sustain me. It quenches my thirst from the top down, filling me with something more than just a temporary high. It's what gives me a reason to wake up in the morning with a purpose to live for and by, which is what we all we want in the end.

Addiction

The root of our addictions might be our thought life. The way to get wrong thoughts out is to get right thoughts in. Your mind cannot be unoccupied. If you don't occupy your mind with good thoughts, the enemy will fill it with bad ones. Paul urges us as Christians to do our utmost in feeding our minds with goodness because it edifies every area of our life from the inside out. We need to think about what we're thinking about. If you change the things you allow your mind to dwell on, 'God, who makes everything work together, will work you into his most excellent harmonies' (Philippians 4:9 MSG). Part of me secretly enjoyed being addicted: the excitement of it all, regardless of the pain inflicted on myself and those around me. My addiction was a bizarre dichotomy. Even though part of me loved the fact that I could submit and let go of my unwanted obsession, the other part of me liked the control I had in objectifying women. It's part of the rush to let one's fantasies run wild the way we want them to. It was a weird tension. I had to surrender the illusion of control. And to make matters even more confusing—to indeed be free of something which felt freeing—I had to surrender complete control of my life. Instead of submitting to my addiction, I had to submit to God, because when I genuinely do, a beautiful release happens. I stop believing the lies and doubt; I start to feel less compelled to give in to something void of truth. After all, this is what addiction is: a lie.

8

THE TRUTH ABOUT THE FOX WHO LIED

THERE ISN'T A RIGHT WAY TO LIE. BELIEVING otherwise is a lie in itself. You can become good at lying, but, even then, is it possible to believe in it yourself? The thing about lying is that you know full well that you're doing it. Telling the truth is easy because you don't have to think about it; it just is what it is. But lying takes practice; it's hard work because you have to swim upstream against the current of truth. Like a slippery salmon, you're stubbornly doing everything possible to convince whomever that a river runs upstream. Eventually you fool yourself into believing that if you got away with it once, you can do it again. It suddenly gets easier and easier, until lying becomes your truth and you cannot tell the difference anymore. Lying is in the arsenal of those who want to keep things hidden. It helps preserve the addiction, avoid confrontation, maintain denial, and justify the crutch. Addiction not only reprograms your brain, but it also schools you into becoming a professional liar.

This book is the truth about the lie I was living with for years. As with any bad habit, it took me a while to wean myself from avoiding the truth. The hardest part of lying for me wasn't the deceptive, manipulative exchange of information with someone else, but convincing myself first. I had to believe in the lie before I could put it into practice.

A good illustration of this is one of Aesop's popular fables, 'The Fox and the Grapes.' It's a story about a fox that stumbles across a bunch of appetising grapes one afternoon while walking in the forest. Although the grapes were hanging over a lofty branch, a few attempts at jumping and missing them proved it was impossibly high to reach. Even though they were ripe and in season, the fox's frustration started to get the better of him, and he slowly convinced himself that they were too sour to eat. It's easy to despise what you can't have. The fox went through a journey of post-rationalisation, convincing himself of a lie to avoid a painful truth. When you lie, you are sly, just like a fox.

You might be a good person with the best intentions at the time yet still believe that the lie you've just told isn't wrong. This is what psychologists refer to as cognitive dissonance: holding two contradictory beliefs at the same time. Dissonance was cultivated in me at an early age. As a pubescent teenager, I had a fairly strict religious upbringing where any sexual exploration was discouraged. The standard in my home was extremely conservative, so my pursuit of any counter beliefs meant that I had to work twice as hard at convincing myself that despite a difference in opinion, it didn't automatically mean I had bought a one-way ticket to hell. My fear of disappointing God still looms over me today. By the time I was dating and eventually married, my warped sexual behaviour felt normal. For years I lived a double life with two opposing truths constantly wrestling to pin the other down. Only one was ever going to win.

When you spend enough time living a lie, you quickly learn how to justify it. I was amazed at how easily I managed to rationalise my behaviour as acceptable. I spent years wearing my mind down until I couldn't think otherwise. I was caught in a vicious circle. Like a merry-go-round at a carnival, it was impossible for me to jump off at any time I chose. Instead I would fall back on tried and trusted rebuttals whenever I messed up: 'Oh, I did it because I had a bad day at work.' 'I'm just in a weird mood and don't really feel myself.' 'I've got a lot going on in my life at the moment.' None of these ever made me feel any better. They were quick shots of proverbial whiskey, excuses barrelled and matured for years, ready to be uncorked, and swigged down the hatch to numb the pain. Still, I would mooch around, disappointed in myself. I was an angry individual. It got to a point where my behavioural signs felt so rehearsed that I acted them out with ease.

My wife soon caught on to this and knew that my sudden anger directly correlated to my shame hangover. She'd always call me out by firing a quick shot: 'Have you looked at porn recently?' I felt like a crook too weak to run. It helped to back-pedal towards her with my hands held up. She's been an absolute rock, and I'm so thankful for how she often kept me accountable when no one else would. But it didn't always keep me from being a repeat offender. My body and mind usually never agreed on giving up so easily. And I still carried the skills of deception.

Despite being aware of the warning signs of my behaviour, I'd still try to figure out a way to mask them from setting off any alarm bells. Usually I was convinced I could stay one step ahead of my wife. But before this became obvious to her or even to me, I would deal with the guilt of my addiction through self-mortification. I would retreat in my shame and sorrow by subjecting myself to worship songs all day to the point that my house felt like a Hillsong convention. Alternatively, if I failed at conjuring my happy-clappy self to a better me, I'd lash out in anger at whoever was in my path that day. Feeling this way would always attract punishment from the world and also create it for me. Projecting my anger onto others was inadvertently showing disappointment in myself. I was looking for a fight but picking it with the wrong person. Neither form of amercement could cover my guilt and shame. All it did was create a false sense of atonement that spiralled into a vicious cycle. The truth is, you'll never feel as though you've been sufficiently punished.

If you've ever watched the film *The Mission,* it touches heavily on this theme. I've always resonated with the protagonist in Roland Joffe's acclaimed film. In English class in high school we would watch a scene every Tuesday morning, analyse and discuss it. The story is peppered in symbolism, which is why we studied it as part of our curriculum. The two main characters represent human character. One is hope, played by Jeremy Irons—a Spanish Jesuit who ventures into the deepest, darkest jungle in South America to provide promise through the gospel. The other is a slave hunter who brings despair to the people, played by Robert De Niro. The short of it is that good naturally triumphs evil, and De Niro's character realises what he is doing is wrong and joins Irons in his mission. Part of his 'conversion' is his penance, which seems to take up much of the film. For the most part, it's a visual metaphor as we witness his journey through the jungle with a heavy rock chained to his feet, slowly ascending a steep mountain. It reminded me of the parallel imagery of the Via Dolorosa 'Way of Suffering,' where Christ carried the sins of the world on the way to his crucifixion. Just like Christ, when they try to relieve De Niro's character of the unbearable weight, he refuses. He believes his pain is what's needed to cover the guilt and shame.

Shame and guilt are what kept me continually locked up, and they perpetuated the lies I used to conceal from others and, more importantly, what I used to say about myself, others, and God. I say this because in order to understand a lie, you must understand guilt and shame. One of my wife's more forgivable vices was a routine practice: when she had a bad day at work she'd automatically reach for anything in the cupboards covered in chocolate. And, I mean anything. She wasn't investing in Cadbury because the chocolates released all kinds of serotonin goodness. The creamy row of chocolate heaven tiles was something more. A reliable source of consolation tucked in purple foil and ready to be opened when life had let her down. Reaching for familiarity offers a sense of security in an unpredictable life. The whole 'I might as well' attitude seems to soften the shame because the shame is what lets you believe the lie that this is what you need to feel better again, and then, feeling sick after finishing the slab plays on the guilt of the aftermath. The disgust in how she felt translated into the shame in how she believed she looked. A cycle which would play out all over again. It's a trivial analogy, but you can sympathise how shame, self-hatred, and self-loathing all grow to a point where you become inwardly focused on what you are not instead of the truth of what the Creator has designed you to be. Equally, if you continually allow your thoughts to be directed by the guilt of your short-comings, they'll eventually become a fortress of shame. It's important to realise the difference between failing and believing you are a failure. You are not your individual sins. The apostle Paul wrestles with this internal battle in the book of Romans. He admits to being consumed with not sinning as opposed to doing good. Being held captive by a fear of failure, piling the guilt on himself, making him fearful of separation from God, he laments, 'What a wretched man I am!' Again, his guilt has transpired to shame. It takes Paul a long time to realise guilt should be used as a positive response and reminder to run to God and that shame always directs you in the opposite direction.

Religion didn't shine a light on things for me; instead, it kept me hidden in the darkness of shame. I never felt 'set free,' I felt like a disappointment. It had a pharisaic rather than liberating effect on me. It was more about the dos and the don'ts, so my childhood was spent feeling so scared of anything to do with sex, including the opposite sex. I often wonder if this had an adverse effect on me. My whole concept of intimacy was a fruit salad of varying beliefs. It was more of a mystery to me than enlightenment. It carried a certain awe and enchantment. Nothing was demystified for me, only subjugated. The more any thought or action was countered, the greater I learned to fear it, spiralling my curiosity even more. I now realise my fear of sex led to a paralysing conviction of worthlessness and shame. These lies became my inner core beliefs for years. I often wonder how things might have turned out had I not been so anxious about sex.

I had a friend whose mother gave her condoms at the age of fourteen. When I was fourteen I had no idea what its purpose was, so the idea of sex was about as foreign as a vegan barbecue. I know times have changed and fourteen now is like dog years, but I can assure you, no one I knew at my age was packing a rubber next to their pocket money in their luminous Velcro wallet. Sure, there might have been kissing and touching, but that was about as risqué as it would get. Any mother who dishes out an accordion of square-shaped foil wrappers to her teenage daughter has already had a detailed chat about the birds and the bees. So when she closed her daughter's palm over into a fist for safekeeping, it was a symbolic gesture for demysti-fying the inevitable. I can't say I know this girl's sexual history, but what I can say is any fear associated with sex had been dismantled. Her mother felt it didn't need to be something awkward or frowned on. Is it great parenting? I'll leave that for you to decide. From past conversations with my friend, I know she always felt comfortable enough to talk to her mother about anything most kids wouldn't dream mentioning. This analogy is one extreme. I don't think I would've traded all my naiveté. I had a pretty sound understanding around the importance of sex within marriage, but the beauty of it was clouded by the fear of overemphasis. It would've helped not to have anxiously approached it the way I did, to the point of feeling overwhelmed for years.

I vividly recall one particular scenario in primary school. I was at a house party, and my friend's parents had built a 'granny flat' at the back of their property. It didn't house any grandparents yet, but it would often be used as a convenient retreat from the main house. That particular Friday evening, most of the boys conveniently used it as a place to sneak off to with girls. I remember one of my friends taking a girl he fancied there. The rest of us would gather outside the window, eavesdrop, listening intently and occasionally letting out high-pitched giggles like school girls. We imagined all the naughty things they were doing, mostly hyperbolic theories thrown around from the less experienced.

Word on the playground was that they never had sex, but they did fool around. I never fully understood the concept of 'fooling around,' which left me anxious about knowing the proper etiquette if I were ever faced with such a situation. No one showed me. Just like in the movies, the word 'base' was often thrown around. 'Did you get to second base or third base?' I had no idea what the hierarchy represented. In a country where the game of cricket was played, I had a vague understanding of bases but failed to connect the symbolic dots. The navigational sporting analogy was lost on me. Sure, I had older brothers to help explain these pubescent conundrums, but it's not like they had a detailed handbook with footnotes to hand over. Standing outside the window, as intriguing as it was, confused and frightened me even more. I was too embarrassed to ask, which only compounded my anxiety. Every kid gets it wrong as they fumble through life. Our imaginations run wild, so it's not out of the ordinary to embellish uncertainty.

I'm reminded of a scene from one of my favourite movies, *Singles*, because it brilliantly paints the many insecurities and inaccuracies of romantic love against a grungy backdrop. One of the main characters, who reflects on being a young boy, tells a story of a time when he was sitting in a doctor's office learning about intercourse. Naturally, he's freaked out by the doctor's graphic candour and inadvertently mishears an important piece of information, later retelling a slightly distorted version to his friends on the edge of the basketball court: "And what squirts out of a man's penis during intercourse is Spam." They all squirm, 'Ewwww' (Yes, the tinned meat).

I learned at a very young age how to justify my actions, and part of the justification involved becoming a master of deception. What I thought to be a strength was nothing more than a lie covering up a weakness. I had convinced myself that the lie I was living was the truth. If you don't call out deception early—if you don't tell people and seek the right kind of help—it only becomes more powerful and impossible to avoid. There's something quite liberating that happens when you choose to open up: your addiction instantly loses power. It doesn't necessarily go away completely, but its grip loosens considerably. Although certain signs of my addiction were visible to me, I failed to notice how I increasingly became deceitful as my addiction grew stronger, to the point where I would find the most ingenious ways of deceiving everyone around me. At times I would make excuses as to why I was late to work or meeting up with friends. I would turn my phone off or put my family's calls on silent. Important, healthy moments were usually sucked up by time spent living out my lies. The more I deceived, the deeper I fell. I was such a convincing liar who lied so much that I honestly can't remember having ever lied.

Anyone with an addiction is a liar. That's some cold, hard truth. You're either lying to yourself or to a loved one. If you're the latter, it might take a massive slip up for the truth to be revealed. Not everyone is going to have a scandalous politician moment where they're found in a hotel room with a prostitute and a bag of smack in their lap. For some people addiction is insidious; they feed it at home, behind closed doors, behind a computer screen. As technology progresses it will increasingly be impossible to disconnect from the internet. Everybody will be hiding behind a screen. The only way to root out this kind of addiction is by calling it what it is. If not, it will rise to the surface eventually, whether your relationship with your wife wanes, or you lose interest at work, or your guilt turns into depression. Every time I conserved my addiction, I picked up a brick, and one by one I built a wall of lies between me and anyone who mattered. Every brick blocked intimacy in my relationships until there was no way in. I felt like my identity was robbed, but when I started to take a step back and sniff out where the dissonance lurked, only then was I in a much better position to straighten my mind out. I realised the lies would stop only when I stopped dwelling on the guilt and allowing the roots of shame to bury deeper into my soul. And the enemy of my soul wanted me to be in a continuous state of malaise, too exhausted to know or seek the truth. It took me a long time to work through the lies I had convinced myself to be true and to eventually reject them. Identifying them was key to my journey in reframing them to God's truth.

Deception

There are two types of lies: lies you tell yourself and lies you tell others. I spent years wrestling with the two. Like Paul, I tried everything in my power to prevent myself from slipping. But it never worked. It's because the whole 'works' thing doesn't work. Convincing myself that I had to be clean to become good was nothing more than a big lie. And when you feel dirty, it's a destructive response initiated by shame and guilt that urges you to run from God instead of towards him. We all know it's not what the gospel is about. The story of the gospel is about coming as you are: dirty, broken, desperate. I remember hearing a talk by author Philip Yancey, in it he recounted one illustration which never left me: when we are broken, at our lowest point, we're like a child coming indoors from playing in the mud and dirt outside. Expecting the mother to scream and shout, she doesn't, but does the opposite instead. She runs a bath for her child to wash and clean because she knows it's a seldom opportunity for her to wrap a towel around her child and hold on tight. Just like God's love, when we're dirty that's when we're closest to him. Good works won't keep out the bad. The only way you can change your actions is by changing your beliefs—changing the way you think about yourself, changing the way you see your relationships, and recognising you don't need to hide your sin in shame and guilt.

9

THE ART OF DISTRACTION

A distraction is not a distraction unless you pay attention to it.

— ANONYMOUS

MOST WELL-STUDIED PASTORS HAVE A PROPENSITY TO name drop C. S. Lewis to illustrate a sermon. It would be remiss not to do the same as he fits rather snuggly with the theme in this chapter. Undoubtedly one of the theological giants of our time, his effortless, mercurial style captures everyone from children to scholars. Surprisingly, Narnia wasn't my first introduction to Lewis, nor was the influential *Mere Christianity*. One epistolary novel I discovered early on, from his exhaustive catalogue, was *The Screwtape Letters*. I found this satirical masterpiece devilishly funny despite Lewis's claim that it was unenjoyable to write and he resolved never to pen another letter. Perhaps he intended the book's debate to be taken seriously instead of being adapted into plays, a comic book, and an audio drama. It might never make it on the Bible study curriculum, but all those who have read it can agree that it packs plenty of food for thought, mirroring human life with all its shortcomings in a theatrical way. It brilliantly provides a series of lessons used to address the everyday Christian ethical and moral dilemmas we often face but are too flawed to resist. Once you look past the absurdity of two demon pen pals, Screwtape and Wormwood, corresponding in letters to one another, you begin to appreciate the whimsical yet relevant way these two characters address the Christian theological issue of temptation.

The art of seduction is a theatrical dance in itself— a well-rehearsed choreography of mankind wrestling with the day-to-day challenges of life. A letter I found particularly sublime in its application to all Christians trying to 'walk the walk' was Screwtape's conversation with his nephew, Wormwood, about distraction as the best lure for temptation. He cleverly points out that the greatest magic trick of all is the ability to capture man's wandering attention to 'something or even nothing at all.' Achieve this, and it'll be more than sufficient, so long as it keeps a man away from any time spent of great value:

You no longer need a good book, which he really

likes, to keep him from his prayers or his work or his sleep; a column of advertisements in yesterday's paper will do. You can make him waste his time not only in the conversation he enjoys with people whom he likes, but in conversations with those he cares nothing about on subjects that bore him. You can make him do nothing at all for long periods. You can keep him up late at night, not roistering, but staring at a dead fire in a cold room. All the healthy and outgoing activities which we want him to avoid can be inhibited and nothing given in return, so at last he may say, as one of my own patients said on his arrival down here, 'I now see I spent most of my life in doing neither what I ought nor what I liked.'[1]

Distraction is the devil's greatest pastime. Turn back to the textual history of the creation of man: the familiar story in the garden of Eden and the resplendent apple on the tree, its taut skin gleaming in the morning sun. The thought of biting into its honey-crisp flesh too delicious and impossible to ignore. Even though we know there was more to the 'forbidden apple'—which wasn't flavoured with the sweetness of sin but instead was symbolic of man's battle with temptation—it began with a simple distraction. Today is no different. We are surrounded by shiny apples just waiting to be eaten. Screwtape knows this, so he sheds light on how easy it is and how foolish we are. He illuminates Wormwood:

> You will be gradually freed from the tiresome business of providing Pleasures as temptations. As the uneasiness and his reluctance to face it cut him off more and more from all real happiness, and as habit renders the pleasures of vanity and excitement and flippancy at once less pleasant and harder to forgo (for that is what habit fortunately does to a pleasure) you will find that anything or nothing is sufficient to attract his wandering attention.[2]

It's so true: a distraction isn't beholden to pleasure. A distraction is a diversion, whether it's fun or not. So long as it does the job, it's a job done.

When I first read this letter, it was like eavesdropping on the enemy's battle plans. It's so obvious in hindsight, as hindsight always is. But we don't fully see it for what it is in the moment. Most are probably aware of being distracted, but only a handful can spot it creeping up. If you asked me what the greatest weapon of evil is, I wouldn't point to a conspicuous bunker in North Korea. I would say it's a distraction. Distraction is the inlet to sin where your wandering mind begins to drift down a steady stream, eventually washing you away in a fast-flowing cascade of rapids, knocking you about until you're pulled under. It's an invitation for temptation; in fact, it is a form of temptation. It's the greatest weapon used to keep us away from God. Every day we're fighting distractions. You were sidetracked by a conversation after work and couldn't make it in time for dinner; you went out late the night before and couldn't get up for church; the game was too riveting to miss, so your wife sat in the other room feeling unloved. We've all been there. I know I've watched many sports games while my wife reluctantly found something else to do. They were only a few of the day-to-day distractions for me.

There's also a distraction which has the power to cleverly fool you every time—beckoning to move in a little closer, inviting you to take one peek, to gently dip your toe in, to take a sweet bite. A distraction that is eventually coerced into a habit. My descent never happened overnight for me. I didn't wake up one morning with an unhealthy sexual appetite. Over time my mind fed my desires more and more until this hunger was accepted as normal. I'm sure many can relate. The temptation to cater to this desire is not exactly easy to avoid. It's all around us. From the moment we wake up and fumble for our phones, to the morning commute where we navigate through the fog of commercial products that vie for our attention and get louder as the day goes on. Thousands of things compete for our attention each day. Amongst the noise is an industry milking as much of our engagement as possible. In turn this distraction has festered a hyper-sexuality within us, fuelled by the ever-increasing amount of sexually suggestive imagery served up every day. One no longer needs to go looking for it; it comes to you wherever you are. The choice and susceptibility are far greater now. It's not uncommon for six-year-olds to walk around school grounds with a mobile phone in their trouser pocket. When I was young (not to sound like an old man), I had to go to the corner café for a naughty sneak peek, and even then it was impossible and awkward. The only magazine available back then was a local publication called *Scope*—everybody knew it because the ladies' privates were concealed with stars that looked like a supermarket starburst sale sign. This only left more to the imagination.

Distraction, whatever the subject, is without prejudice. It targets anyone it can. A recent article I read highlights how the temptation of distraction is heightened because of the digital age. Our hourly social fix is greatly affecting our mental health—leading to anxiety, depression, sleep deprivation, and body-image issues in young people. We trawl through thousands of images and posts of other people, living vicariously through their lives instead of getting on with living our own. I find it incredibly difficult and exhausting to stay focused. From the garish pornographic popup banners appearing unexpectedly in our browser to a titillating advert in a magazine, all of a sudden it's impossible to ignore, and you begin to fixate without realising you are.

This is where distraction ignites the fuse of arousal.

It's like when an outlaw lays dynamite in an old Western movie. He strikes a match and lights the longest fuse, allowing him just enough time to crouch behind a nearby rock or wagon and then—KABOOM! It's how sexual temptation works. Every time my eyes scan an image, whether it's intended or not, a fuse is lit. The more fuses that are lit, the bigger the boom and inevitably the greater the damage. So even though aimlessly checking out some girl out at the super-market might seem harmless, a fuse has been lit.

It's tiresome work to stamp out every fuse, but it can be done. The first step is not to brush it off as harmless fun or think that, 'it's nothing to worry about.' Whenever I walk into a doctor's waiting room, I become hyper-aware of the magazines that are laid out and avoid picking them up for fear of what I might see. It sounds paranoid, but I know that seeing a fitness magazine with a bikini-clad girl on the cover is a distraction for me. A subtle impression like that could trigger unhealthy thoughts later. Although it's natural to write off a magazine as a silly distraction, it vexed me for years, and when I caught myself being distracted by these kinds of things, I realised that there were times I had looked at it longer than I thought, perhaps even twice. A simple magazine cover is just one tiny example of how distraction works. It's just another fuse. For some men it might just be a long fuse that takes forever to burn and probably diminishes; for others, it might be pretty short, igniting enough force to kick you into temptation. For many of my friends it certainly started this way as young boys.

Fighting distraction is impossible when idle. It's the devil's recess. Idle time leads to distraction, which leads to temptation. I know myself pretty well by now, and if I am not busy or focused on something, I'm easily swayed and vulnerable to temptation. Once my mind slips, it's almost impossible to reverse. It's like a scene out of a movie where someone driving a car tries to slow down by pumping the brakes. They pump and pump the pedal, but nothing happens. There's a quick cut to a shot of the tampered brakes, then back to a close-up of a startled face. We all know how this movie cliché ends (unless, of course, it's Chuck Norris driving). It's all out of control from there, and this is what it's pretty much like for me.

Distraction doesn't patiently wait in the wings for you to announce its entrance. It will appear sporadically and when it pleases; it knows to pounce at the least expected moment. I'd be jogging home after work, listening to a Christian podcast, and some flashy mirage would catch the corner of my eye. Before I knew it—BAM! I'd find myself at home on my computer scouring the internet, hours later, topping up my senses. I often couldn't tell how I jumped from A to Z. I would utterly have no clue. It felt like a scenario out of *Quantum Leap*, the early nineties sci-fi show. The protagonist, Sam Beckett, would instantly be shifted through time and appear in a random year. He would always have a startled look of 'What the heck just happened, and how did I get here?' It's what getting sucked into the vortex of sexual addiction felt like for me. I felt enslaved and oblivious to the passing of time. In Proverbs there's a verse which references a 'lust that takes you captive'. This tug of war between master and servant became a common theme for me. I'm sure most people have felt a similar pull. But even if you have the ability to stall the distraction by refraining from acting on it, the war is by no means won. It will wait, sitting dormant, until an opportune moment to steal your attention arises. If you don't deal with problems in the moment, they will inevitably find a way of catching up with you.

We all know the familiar Bible story of King David's temptation. If anyone was susceptible to distraction, it was him. David, during a stressful time and most likely full of decision making, was sidetracked. All it took was a couple of looks one evening, and the imprinted imagery began to fester in an unhealthy way. As the most powerful man in the kingdom of Israel and Judah, David was certainly used to getting what he wanted. His lust wasn't waning or fleeting, but stirring. He didn't cut it off; instead, he let it linger. It was as if David was welcoming the distraction: a pleasant and alluring intermission to the chaotic and demanding stage play of his life. He could've acted like Joseph, who fled from Potiphar's wife. David's case seemed mild compared to Joseph's. Joseph had a woman literally grabbing him by the hand and throwing herself at him. David merely saw a woman changing out of the corner of his eye.

This is often how distraction works. David was caught off guard, whereas Joseph was focused and aware. Distraction also comes at a time when it knows it can entice. David, whose men were in the midst of battle, most likely found looking at Bathsheba calming on his senses and an escape from reality. At the time it couldn't have been any further from the decisions of war. But I highly doubt David would have paused to dance with lady lust had he caught a glimpse of her mid-battle. The question is, as he stood on the balcony looking out under the night sky, was there a part of him that willed distraction? Was he searching for something to lose himself in? Is there a part of us that wills distraction? Most of my battles with lust have been due to distraction. I'm distracted because a big part of me silently wishes to step out on a balcony. It's not because I long to be with the person embodying my lust but because I seek anything that'll alleviate the stress and pressures of life. Why is it that when we read about politicians or people high up in the corporate ladders of life, men in power like David, they too confess to their own Bathsheba moments? Their shiny apple, harmless in appearance, offering a temporary distraction from the responsibilities of life. Desperate to be edified, the soul is tricked by a weak mind into believing that that which is fleeting is sustainable. Lewis's *Screwtape Letters*, veiled in Wormwood's words, insightfully illustrates the devil on our shoulder: the whisper in our ears and the taunting to temptation, but beneath the comedy is a haunting reminder of a war raging within. When we lose focus, we inevitably lose our will to live the life we're called to live.

Temptation

I have spent a good part of my life arm wrestling with distraction and have inevitably lost. Over the years, I have trained myself to be more vigilant, still guarding my heart as much as possible, controlling what I can. It's exhausting, but no one ever said taking up the cross and following Christ would be easy. Paul wrote in Ephesians about clothing yourself in the armour of God. I always thought this was a goofy activity because Sunday school always made us create ours out of paper, with the option to add a splash of crayon. For Christian kids, your mom bought you either a He-Man figurine or, if she refused (like mine did), a Bible Man. Why? Well, because Bible Man was customised with the armour of God: Helmet of Salvation, Belt of Truth, Sword of the Spirit, Breastplate of Righteousness—many battle-resistant features. As much as I joke about it now, the image of Bible Man has never left me. It showed someone who was ready to battle. Not someone who was invincible, but someone prepared. Half the battle of distraction, temptation, and addiction is arming yourself every day before these can play out. I never fully understood the importance of preparing for battle until I realised how afflicted I'd become. It sounds so melodramatic, but your opinion is bound to change when you come home every day feeling defeated. I know that if I let my guard slip, I'm prone to affliction. It doesn't mean you have to stand in front of the mirror every morning running through an itemised arsenal checklist, but the metaphor is there to remind you that at any point in time you might be hit by a stray arrow. I urge you to make it a priority every day to prepare for spiritual warfare. I know that if I haven't dwelled on Jesus's words and implemented them in my daily life, I have no waypoint and will find myself aimlessly wandering down a road with no idea how I got there.

10

DOWN THE HABIT HOLE

Failure is simply the opportunity to begin again, this time more intelligently.

— HENRY FORD

LAST NIGHT MY SEXUAL ADDICTION WON. FOR A WHILE I felt as if I had slowly been making progress, only to lose my footing, and the hard yards I had gained. I was disappointed. I am exhausted from ascending and defending the mental cliff face I clung to in my mind, a familiar solo attempt I knew all too well. 'I had come this far', I thought, 'no point turning back now.' The temptation was a rush I couldn't resist, so I answered the mountain's call and set off while my wife slept at the proverbial base camp of our bed.

My demise began earlier while sitting on the couch watching *Mission Impossible: Ghost Protocol.* I was a little bored, having seen it a couple of times, so I grabbed my wife's phone and randomly browsed the internet at the point where Tom 'I do all my own stunts' Cruise attempts the impossible ascent, using some magical sensory adhesive gloves to scale the Burj Khalifa. I watched as he nonchalantly scuttled across the glass surface. My eyes flicked up and down, moving between two screens vying for my attention. The television held my attention for a few moments longer, just as Tom reached the floor where he sliced open the window like a cookie cutter and arched through the hobbit-like hole inside. In the spirit of heightened drama, 700 metres roughly speaking, his left glove loses its mechanical grip. The weight of his body is too much for one hand, causing him to slide a few stories down before managing to get some kind of contact with the glass, preventing him from falling any further. I couldn't stomach watching him single-hand-edly make his way back up, even if it's Tom Cruise. Ironically, what could have been used as some life lesson wasn't enough to stop me from losing my own grip with every tap of the phone. Every device in my house has a parental lock, barring my wife's phone, so holding it was like holding Pandora's box (which, as I write this is, has since been locked).

I knew full well that what I was doing was wrong. I say this because in these moments it's important to point out my awareness of the choices I make. I'm not sporadically hypnotised into doing something I don't want to do, which raises the question: If you're aware that what you're doing is wrong, why pick the wrong choice in the first place? But what I often knew to be wrong wasn't enough to outweigh the evidence of going with what's right. The wrong decision doesn't always immediately feel wrong, which is why temptation is so alluring. Often the exhilaration of dipping my toe into forbidden waters has seemed overpowering. In the moment of a sweetened whisper I would shudder with excitement, entranced by the siren's call. The illuminated glaze of the computer screen would beckon me towards a kaleidoscope of seductive imagery, drawing me closer to her whispers of unwanted thoughts. Before I knew it, I was drowning—staring at online cam girls as they paraded like mannequins in a virtual shop window. The rush of dopamine increased with the pop-up of every new window. To keep the floodgates of visual candy open, each click must exceed the next. While conscious of what I was feeding my mind, I remained impervious to thoughts of the long-term side effects.

In moments of heightened sexual provocation, reason has hardly ever made an appearance. My frontal lobe was sidelined before the game of logic versus lust even kicked off. I always thought that being in a loving, healthy relationship would finally make me impervious to teenage sexual misgivings. It didn't. My sin only pained me more because now it wasn't just me in the picture: I was hurting someone else. Like Newton's third law of motion, my sinful actions inadvertently would recoil and impact our marriage. Did I think about God leading up to my demise? No, not really; however, I did feel slightly convicted as I went along. On one shoulder I had the whisper of moral conscience, on the other a cry of exuberance encouraging me to lose control completely (just this once, of course). It often has felt like a much heavier weight at times, like large looming forces at play.

My mind naturally conjured invisible spiritual battles between light and dark waging above me. It's like a cover I once saw at the church bookstore that simultaneously intrigued me and freaked me out. It was Frank E Perreti's *This Present Darkness*. On it, the image of an ominous claw-like silhouette formed from a blackened cloud which loomed over a small village like something from an M Night Shyamalan movie. My mind felt like it was in an eternal mental grip that was impossible to escape. I couldn't see past the dark clouds that flanked me. All I could hear was the metal-on-metal swish of swords cutting through the air around me. Although these thoughts were commonplace, evoking feelings of insignificance, they were often part of my internal process—a visual inclination met with a visual invocation. I would often think this way, and, because of it, I was inevitably left bruised, wounded, pierced with guilt. At times I still feel let down by how the good within me has failed to persevere. I would argue with God, questioning why he couldn't send down some bigger angel as firepower, or why the Holy Spirit didn't strengthen me to withstand the blows. I felt like a proverbial pawn making a wrong move and paying for it with an eternal checkmate.

For years, I naturally assumed that just because I was a Christian (or at least considered myself one), I was in line for some sort of respite. I would be allowed just enough temptation to eventually claim victory. This kind of thinking, however, was naive. I felt cheated by a Scripture I had always clung to as my mantra when times were tough, the familiar cushion of 1 Corinthians 10:13 (NIVUK): 'No temptation has overtaken you except what is common to mankind. And God is faithful; he will not let you be tempted beyond what you can bear. But when you are tempted, he will also provide a way out so that you can endure it.' I have never been able to decode this verse to prevent my life from falling into recurring entropy. Scriptural sentimentality is dangerous because you can use it to justify any action. I know I have, often along the lines of:

- If we're tempted in the same way as everyone else, then why are some tempted more than others?
- If I've just sinned, then God couldn't have

been present, because if he were, he
wouldn't have let me battle with something
far greater than my own strength.

- If God had been part of this, why would he
allow me to sin in the first place?
- Sure, there's free will, but if my will is
overpowered, why do I need free will in the
first place?
- If I sin because of the overpowering force
of temptation, yet he's promised never to
allow me to be tempted to the point of
defeat, then why do I feel defeated?
- Surely my sinful act isn't my fault if it's too
much for me to handle.
- If God allows only temptations that we can
handle, then by that logic we would never
find ourselves in a situation where
temptation has got the better of us, because
we'd always be victors.

These musings would continuously circle my mind
like a dog chasing its tail. I think therein lies the
danger, and it's something we seem to do a lot of in the
Christian community: hang on to Scriptures like medic-
inal recipes passed down from our mother's great-
grandmother, like some sort of magical elixir. Truth is,
I don't believe it's what the Author intended. In reality,
my battle is commonplace. It's not exclusive to me.
Every day, all over the world, people are experiencing

the exact same temptations and transgressions that I am. My experiences might vary, but the sin is no different. So even though I'm battling the seemingly impossible alone, I'm really not. And God gets this. Temptation isn't a new concept to him—it was prevalent throughout the Bible. It's common to humanity and it's no different now. Paul isn't telling the church of Corinth that God will deflect any bothersome nuisance that tries to gain access to our minds, like some sort of burly bouncer outside a nightclub. He's offering assurance within the gift of free will: there are common solutions to common problems. Your defeat at the hands of sin isn't any greater than the victory claimed. In other words, the possibility is as strong as the impossible. It's not impossible to resist as much as it's possible to give in to sin. When I look back on my life, I am angry at my lack of faith and discipline in seeking solutions. There were areas in my life I had overlooked. I wasn't always staying connected to God's words and wisdom for my life.

The parable of the vine illustrates this beautifully. A vine needs a central point to wrap around and intertwine in a constant direction. Without a central anchor, the vine can be nourished only from its own strength. I have struggled and relied on my own devices, my own strength, far too much. Understanding this helped me make sense of Paul's words in Philippians where he spent many days and nights in prison, having been falsely charged and mistreated, yet affirming the hope that we can do all things through Christ who strengthens us. Paul understands that hope is found not in his own devices but in seeking guidance and direction in Christ. Giving up control is not a sign of weakness, but a sign of strength.

———————

I went to bed feeling disgraced and with an enormous sense of separation from any offering of grace. The aftereffects had left a dense residue on my soul that slowly seeped into other areas of my life, particularly my marriage. It always did. The next morning when I woke, every word that left my mouth carried undertones of hostility, with the slightest provocation setting me off. My wife would sense a distance and feel the recoil from my aggression. I couldn't bear to look at her. When we kissed, it felt as strange as kissing my grandmother on the lips. A friendly peck but nothing more. There could be nothing more. All my emotions were numb. I had no right to offer love. I was castigating myself but making my wife pay for my transgressions. With any addiction, you peak at a dramatic high only to end at an abysmal low. You experience a real lack of self-worth. If you relate to this, then you've either been on the receiving end of the highs and lows or the subject of a recurring nightmare like mine. Just as my addiction was habitual, so too were the manifestations.

I wish I had a silver bullet to offer you all, but I don't. There is no quick fix, only a process that requires hard work. It isn't insurmountable. We're capable of more than we think, even when we don't think we are. It's important to take the selfish side of our actions and turn them into selfless ones. By doing this we offer up our pride and surrender our lives to something far greater than ourselves. Twelve steps programs now diplomatically refer to it as a Higher Power. I do believe I would've defeated my addictions a lot sooner had I not been utterly selfish in my desires. Recovery is geared towards improving yourself, but not on your own terms. Your own terms are what trapped you in an addictive cycle in the first place.

Guilt and Shame

Grace is the only sufficient impulse that can supersede guilt. If you're supporting someone close to you, it will no doubt require a lot from you. There will be times when your partner slips up and spirals into a guilt-ridden frenzy. This frustration will mean digging deeper. It's inevitable, and it is why healing is a process. Discipline is imperative, but without grace it cannot be implemented. Showing constant support and love might seem like a fleeting gesture, but it won't go unnoticed, and it's often the only source of comfort to your partner in trying times. For those who struggle with addiction, grace comes our way not because of what we do or what we don't do. When we allow grace to permeate within, it transfuses through our veins, fostering a release of self-control and humility. Submission to something bigger than you is key. You are not God. If you were, you wouldn't be reading this; you'd be out saving the world. Recovery is achieved through hard work, support, and positive affirmations in your own life, which will help increase your awareness of the grace you've been given.

11

HOW I CHANNELLED MY INNER TONY ROBBINS

THE GREATEST COST OF MY ADDICTION WASN'T monetary. It was my confidence. The cologne of insecurity seemed to stick to me like a musty smoker's jacket. I grew accustomed to this scent that was impossible to wash off. It wasn't an attractive scent, but I suppose in some way a whiff of self-loathing emanates from all of us. We're imperfect by nature, leaving self-doubt always to remain a constant struggle. For some, it hinders all aspects of life to the point where it's a major disability. It had a paralysing affect on my formative years. Part of growing up is about learning and working on who you want to be in adulthood. Throughout my youth I felt stunted. I hated the thought of having to speak to a stranger. It made me anxious, which became a constant cycle. I would plead with my mother to step in for me when I was too afraid or embarrassed to do so myself. From an early age, I had very little confidence. Top it off with a distorted view of women, and I was inevitably doomed to failure from the outset.

It's impossible for me to say whether my fascination with lust was because of my social anxiety or because it spiralled into a deeper sense of low self-confidence. Perhaps it was a bit of both. If you look at most cases of people who suffer from addiction problems, they are usually considered to be shy and introverted. Their probability of having low self-esteem, in turn, manifests in some sort of substance or emotional abuse, whether it's alcohol, drugs, or gambling. An alcoholic might habitually depend on drink to help combat any awkwardness, to draw them out of their shell, and to offer a level of perceived confidence and gregariousness. Some recognise that alcohol decreases anxiety, which helps fuel a more confident self. In hindsight, I had built all these common tendencies over time, but I never relied on substances as such; instead, I relied on the coping mechanism of humour. Unknown to most, I was feeding a demanding sexual addiction between the cracks and in the quiet.

At this point, it's important to note that exuding confidence doesn't make you automatically immune to addiction. Sometimes overbearing confidence can compensate for more rooted insecurities. You just have to look at congenial comedians to know that the pain they are feeling is contrary to the life they are reflecting. An abundance of self-adulation is often too much for the human brain to comprehend, so it resorts to coping mechanisms. But again, this is the way the pendulum swings: an excess of anything will always lead to a harmful experience.

It's equally safe to say that being introverted doesn't make for a doomed life of addiction. Unfortunately, the word *introvert* immediately draws negative connotations instead of an educated, sympathetic response. After reading Susan Cain's book *Quiet*, I learned how being an introvert is, in fact, a strength in itself. It's important to note that there is a massive difference between low self-esteem and a lack of confidence. The latter would involve a lack of proficiency in one's ability to master, say, the art of golf, hitting the dance floor and tearing it up with your silky-smooth moves, or grabbing a mic and holding the attention of a room for twenty minutes. I would argue that skill is equally coupled with confidence. In my own line of work, I have seen people in power who I don't think are particularly brilliant at their job but who do possess a highly skilled ability to switch on a display of confidence at any given moment. This assurance in themselves is what gets them a lengthy job title to match their six-digit salary. They're not ingenious, but what they do possess is a highly skilled ability to switch on a display to make anyone in the room believe that they are the real deal (when behind the scenes they are as flawed as you and I). If you possess the ability to portray or embellish a sense of confidence, your life could be crumbling around you and no one would be the wiser.

My lack of confidence presented itself as a mental paralysis to being up for any challenge. Low self-esteem is ingrained in the emotional and psychological belief: it inhibits any assurance in a possible positive outcome. Any sense of perseverance is immediately shut down as a futile attempt. I wasn't burdened with low self-esteem from birth; it developed over time. The same is true of my susceptibility to unwanted sexual desires. I wasn't born with it, nor was it fostered by having low self-esteem. I do, however, think that if your confidence is slightly fragile, fallacies can latch onto it like a lion culling a weak animal from the herd. The more I fed my appetite, the harder it attacked my confidence, which inevitably cultivated a sense of low self-esteem. I would often try to anticipate how a situation might unfold, and I'd imagine a million and one ways the scene could play out, creating enough of a case for me not to engage in the first place. The probability of disappointment, leaving me ashamed or dejected, was never worth the investment of 'What if?' I internally jumped ahead to the ending before acting out the beginning and middle. Instead of being in the now and letting life unfold, I had hijacked God's director chair. Part of the reason I gravitated towards dating sites and even towards adult webcams was because there was an element of control in my mind. You knew what you were in for before you even got started, so there was very little room for your feelings to be crushed. I wasn't completely confidence starved; there were other areas of my life where I seemed to still possess a part of it, enough to be convinced it was never an issue. I compartmentalised my ability to handle confronting situations and tried to bury them as deep as I could.

I wouldn't be able to pinpoint the exact moment when my confidence started to take a hit, but in the first few years after leaving high school I was determined to work on it, so I took a job at a magazine publishing company where I learned the art of selling. I was part of a sales team where my day involved cold calling as many potential leads as I could. I had hoped this would help me to front up my insecurities. There's nothing quite as confronting as trying to convince a CEO of a company to cough up a ridiculous amount of money for ad space in a magazine. I learned very quickly that I hated talking to strangers on the telephone, and it took me ages to strike up the nerves to make the first call. My boss, on the other hand, experienced the antithesis of the sickening feeling I felt in my stomach every Sunday night. Every morning he'd be at work an hour earlier, pacing his square-of-a-box office and punching the air while listening to Tony Robbins cassettes. I didn't know who Tony Robbins was at the time, but he sounded like a very angry man whose voice could use a soothing glass of water. I recall a time when we were on our way to close a deal. I was sitting in the passenger seat of his BMW 7-series, and he asked me to hand him a CD from the glove compartment. He slowly popped the disc in and asked if I was ready. I quietly hoped it wasn't Tony Robbins. I fake smiled. And then, instantly the recognisable jolting intro of 'Eye of a Tiger' blasted through his expensive Pioneers. I felt trapped in a bad cliché on wheels. Beads of sweat slowly pooled on his forehead held by the rising creases as he screeched every note. That wasn't even the worst part. I soon was forced to echo his selling mantra of, "ARE WE GOING TO WIN?" with a loud, resounding, "YES, WE ARE." It took me a few goes to sound convincing. Thankfully the drive was short enough to avoid him playing Chumbawamba's 'I Get Knocked Down.' I didn't say a word the whole meeting. On the way back, we drove in silence. We didn't close the deal. I couldn't manufacture confidence; maybe others can. Sales wasn't for me. If I couldn't convince myself, I was never going to convince anyone else.

My low self-esteem didn't come from a loveless place. My home life was nurturing, not chaotic. I was never verbally abused. Raised under a roof of love and righteousness had the opposite effect on me. I believe it contributed to my obsessive need for flirting on the fringes years later. The more my sexual addiction grew, the more my confidence slowly peeled away, a layer at a time, like an onion. It's hard to watch yourself turn from someone who had ambitions and goals, dreams and desires, to someone who settled instead for the status quo. I felt exhausted most of the time; the easy option was always to go with the most comfortable one. Complacency had become part of my everyday existence.

Eventually I moved into a career that I felt suited my personality: advertising. It was creative and interesting enough for me to spend hours with a white A3 pad sketching, brainstorming, and writing up ideas for ads. In the beginning it was super competitive, which spurred on my ambition. I loathed complacency. If I felt I wasn't growing and performing, it was time to move. At thirty-five I had been promoted to Executive Creative Director in a multinational ad agency. I had reached the pinnacle of my career, but the cracks were forming. Initially, I had rejected the promotion. I sat in the boardroom across from my managing director, whose face went from childlike excitement to bewilderment. In my mind, I could hear the advertising community protesting: 'Who in their right mind would ever turn down such a promotion?' 'It's what every creative in the advertising industry works towards, yet only a few are chosen.' But I didn't want it. I didn't want it because I didn't believe I could do it. So I told my managing director that I felt unqualified and needed a few more years in the current role. I didn't; I was scared. I felt too weak to carry such a burden. All I saw were challenges, and I didn't want to rise to them. It was easier to remain seated in a role I already knew. I had kowtowed to the thing I feared most: complacency had become a familiar friend to me instead of a foe. After many debates and lunchtime coffees, I was eventually coaxed into the role.

I surprised myself at how I learned to adapt and command, but my confidence was still at a low point in my life. It eventually caught up with me. I crumbled and left the job and country for a lower-paying role. I wanted to be out of sight and out of mind. To collect my paycheque and head home. It was easier that way, or so I felt. My addiction was calling the shots, not my confidence. I learned to accommodate it in my life so that nothing got in the way. Being in a top management position meant being 100 per cent focused. There was no way my addiction would kindly work part-time. It was demanding when it needed to be. If I had a bad day or my self-worth was criticised, I would automatically gravitate towards something like pornography. It's not as simple as whipping out my laptop every time I had a 'downer'. Something within me gradually culminated in seeking a stimulating escape in whatever way I could. It was reactionary but delayed.

The more I consumed, the more my confidence

waned. With a bit of hindsight, it's easy for me to look back at my career as a timeline of peaks and troughs. I initially responded confidently in various situations, but towards the height of my addiction I retracted and became meek and timid. Today I experience a great deal of frustration because I can clearly see how much I have lost: relationships, time, money, and more.

———————

Objectifying someone takes away all the focus on your own character-building and exerts all your energy towards the person or thing you idolise most. It's as if you strip yourself bare and clothe someone else in all you have, leaving you naked and feeling completely empty. Objectifying women meant I viewed them as a resource, which developed into a habitual production line of supply and demand. My sexual addiction became a full-time venture that demanded my time, worth, capital, relationships, and focus. I had the narcissistic obsession of an entrepreneur. Consumed in my own world, I was the Steve Jobs of my own by-product: iLust.

The reason why the porn industry makes so much money is because of consistency of output. It churns a substantial amount of content 24/7. It never wanes nor sleeps. It never has mood swings or off days. It's ready the moment you are, even when you least expect it. Its omnipresence means you have to be on guard. Porn never demands improvement; it wants you to stay right where you are. It's the reason I never chased after many women. As far as I was concerned, it was hard work. Instead, I grew accustomed to the constant stream of complacency, which eventually flowed through all areas of my life. Progression led to recession. I stopped trying at work. Instead, I opted to stay in the position I knew rather than being involved in unknown or challenging circumstances. The same transpired in my marriage. Things were good but not great. Great meant putting in more effort, which I never did. Just like a builder's spirit level, I was more concerned about keeping things even-keeled instead of looking at the bigger picture.

'Get through it' had become my new mantra: get through the day, get through the week, get through my job, get through my marriage. Just get through it. The problem with this thinking is that it might help you avoid disappointment, but it never offers permanent satisfaction. This is why porn never assuages the emptiness you feel: it will never offer what an authentic relationship can, which is the highs and lows of true intimacy. The more I settled for zero intimacy, the more I was isolated into a world of fear. There was a dichotomy between wanting acceptance and refusing rejection. It took me years to realise I couldn't have both. Life doesn't work this way. Neither do relationships.

I'll never forget when a close friend of mine told me I had 'lost the funny' in a shouty Jerry Maguire way. I was aware how I used to be quite jokey and carefree. I loved humour and took great pleasure in making people laugh. As the years went on, I forgot how to do funny. There was nothing amusing in the world anymore. The candle of laughter was snuffed out. I also had lost any authentic connections. I couldn't distinguish between what was pure and sacred. Women weren't a collection of unique individuals; they were a dehumanised smorgasbord to feast my gluttonous eyes upon. I had consumed an abundance of cheap imitations, leaving me with an indistinguishable, opaque taste. I wouldn't consider myself awkward around women, but there were degrees of uncertainty, especially if objectivity crept in. I would obsess without allowing authenticity to dispel my illusion. It's as if, in a way, I enjoyed the mental dance with the person in my head rather than holding out my hand in a genuine invitation. When I looked beyond the transient figure of pleasure, a more awakened, authentic self developed. Life was no longer a roundabout of instant gratification; it required hard work and offered uncertainty, but the rewards were far more life-changing.

I always knew that walking away from lust required grit and risk. Not only from the abandoned constant but towards the unpredictability of real human interaction. The latter was particularly daunting: being social in real time and not online. The virtual will always remain on the precipice of what's real, but never real enough. Reality is counterintuitive to the way that most of the world accepts a tailored circle of 'friends' without the need ever to be intimate—an inauthenticity in itself, liking the people you deem worthy and declining those you don't.

We live in a culture of blame: we're not encouraged to own responsibility. Instead, we choose to hide behind anonymous avatars and dish out disdain. The username pseudonym was nothing more than an embossed title to prop up on my desk of iniquity and hide behind. I was just another nameless victim floating in the pool of sexual addiction. I convinced myself the plunge wasn't my choice. Surely something from my past inadvertently manipulated me? Aren't I merely a product of my environment? This kind of thinking took me only so far. It convinced me for a while, but even then it sparked a degree of friction with the free will I still had. I couldn't champion autonomy and play the victim. As long as blame is embraced and responsibility is eschewed, the road to recovery will never reveal itself as a plausible path.

My desires were erroneously aimed at myself instead of directing them outwards, towards friends and family for guidance. The more I consumed, the more I had grown inwards—obsessed with my own self, moulding a parochial outlook on life. This only forced me to distance myself even further from friends, compounding my anger. It inflated my self-interest and sunk my problems further down, even more, making it impossible to deal with. I couldn't seem to dig myself out of the hole I had created. How could I if I wasn't recognising the issue I had in the first place? The answer to my problem needed to include a total change in my outlook—a complete reformation of my mind and self-worth and a reinterpretation of true femininity. Once I achieved that, I knew my confidence would start to grow and I would eventually get back to being someone who wouldn't settle for average.

Self-confidence

It's disheartening seeing someone give up so easily. Especially if it's yourself. It's demoralising, and it's how I felt for a very long time. All I know is I lost the feeling and belief in having faith in myself and in my abilities. Somehow, the more I immersed myself in my addiction, the more I lost touch with the world around me. I don't fully understand the science of it all from a qualified perspective, but I know what I've observed through my own experience. As with anything in life, whatever you feed your mind and body, there will be a consequence, whether positive or negative. I knew I wasn't consuming anything good for me spiritually and mentally. I wasn't feeding myself with positive substance to shape and build my character. I lost the desire to read my Bible, to exercise, to eat healthily, to interact and develop relationships—things that make you shine from the inside out. I knew my wife and friends could tell something wasn't quite right in me. I had a cloud above me. I had lost the ability to laugh and be spontaneous, becoming a serious and angry person instead—all defence mechanisms to substitute for a lack of confidence. When you see the fire going out in someone close to you, when you notice something off, it's usually a sign of an internal battle. No one ever really reached out to me, but, to be fair, I didn't make myself accessible. Confidence within comes from filling yourself with things that edify. When you lose your self-belief, you've lost the fight.

12

SIXTY-EIGHT IT

*In long-distance running the only opponent you
have to beat is yourself, the way you used to be.*

— HARUKI MURAKAMI

I PICKED UP A SAYING ONE NIGHT WHILE SHOOTING A
commercial for a nationwide discount retailer. I heard
the assistant director yawp into his walkie-talkie,
commanding one of the junior-ranked grips to 'sixty-
eight' one of the lighting rigs. I've always heard this
term thrown around but never fully understood the
meaning. During one of the many takes, I turned to the
director and softly asked what 'sixty-eight' meant.
'Sixty-ah-ate!' he replied, poorly imitating a Sicilian
accent. He removed his headphones, scrunched his
eyes, and stuck out a pouty lower lip, giving an
awkward Brando-like delivery: "Back in the day, in

Las Vegas, when the mafia needed to whack someone and get rid of the body, they'd drive eight miles out of town." He waited for me to see if I'd get it—I didn't. "You know, it takes eight miles to get to the desert. Cah-peesh?" I got it, finishing his sentence, " . . . And six feet to bury the body." "Bingo Bongo, you goddit!" He pressed his hands on my cheeks, giving me fish lips. All the crew broke into a familiar chuckle like a mob of henchmen laughing at their boss giving this rookie a life lesson. When I think of addiction, I now tell people to "sixty-eight it."

There are two types of quitting. There's the kind where you only give up because you don't believe you have enough mettle. An example of this is what the Marine Corps calls 'hell week,' where a fresh cadet has the opportunity to tap out of the gruelling training at any moment. All he or she must do is voluntarily ring a bell, and they're immediately dismissed. A lot of them won't ring the bell for fear of being labelled a quitter. Then there's the other kind of quitting, which is almost impossible to do: the kind where you would give anything to quit, but you simply don't have the willpower to do it. This type of quitting isn't as immediate as tapping out. It's a more controlled and carefully planned exit strategy. If you believe that ending sexual addiction is as simple as 'pulling up your trousers,' try telling a horny sixteen-year-old to simply cut it out. See how they are after a week, a month, or even a year. Trust me, you will see pain, heartache, and struggle. I know. I've been there.

Initially it was exciting and somewhat controllable, but after a while I would feel antsy and fidgety, unsure of what my body was trying to communicate. I'd soon decipher the screams of this unnatural high, feeling overwhelmed by an insatiable appetite for sexual content. My symptoms were the same as any chemical addiction: varying degrees of sweating, fatigue, foggy brain, and sometimes headaches, I would compulsively rummage through the house in search of any device, picture, or item to satisfy my craving, occasionally substituting heightened fantasies in my mind to do the work.

Relapse was always the same for me. I'd be okay for a day or two and then my brain would send a high-voltage current surging through me and shocking me into a frantic spin. I'd move with mechanical precision. The cycle repeated, again and again. A huge reason for my relapse came down to a lack of preparation on my part. I opened myself to a huge mental battle because I lacked the knowledge of what I was up against. Addiction will never roll over like an obedient dog. A fighting spirit is needed. And when I mean fight, I mean boxing your way to normal—dodging, blocking, punching, and jabbing until there's a KO. And, like any good boxer, being at your personal best requires the wits to outsmart your opponent. Having self-awareness and an understanding of the enemy you're dealing with allows you to put on the gloves of confidence to face your adversary toe-to-toe and go the distance. The biggest thing I've learned about recovery and repentance is that the fight isn't about winning with abstinence. Your success is not about how many 'clean' days you've accumulated. Reducing it to a success rate statistic doesn't touch on the bigger issues of what happens when you relapse. Every time I fought lust, I was fighting for the wrong reason. It just became problem management, grinding through the day, hoping to tick it off my to-do list.

The fight is a creative, existential bout. It's about asking the hard questions of who you want to be. What sort of life do you want to be living? What do you want this year or the next to look like? How would you like today to go? What passion or purpose do you want to pursue? It's about looking forward, not looking back at the days you were lucky enough to be sober. That's a dull existence. A healthy start is to increase your self-awareness (emotional and spatial), making sure you don't get sucker punched by a setback because you weren't keeping an eye on your vulnerabilities.

I know deep down that every time I crossed the line and lusted, no matter the action, whether it was looking at porn or thinking a certain thought, I chose to sin. If I hadn't enjoyed it, I wouldn't have done it in the first place. Sin is attractive and deceptive by nature. Lest we forget, the apple in Eden wasn't full of worms: it was a beautiful, juicy, delicious-looking piece of fruit, enough to make any mouth salivate. Biting into it would've been more appetising. Sometimes we don't even recognise sin for what it is until the aftereffects surface. The first and most important step is identifying it. We must remember that sin obtains its power from our sinning. It looks as appealing as it needs to be to get our attention. Yet it's just as damaging as it is enticing. As much as I may have enjoyed sinning (and I openly did), the repercussions far outweighed the enjoyment. Realising this led to ownership of my sins. If I had never taken responsibility for my grievances, any journey to rehabilitation would've remained dormant.

A good example of owning sin is the familiar historical story of King David—a great leader but with flaws like anyone else. He was the antithesis of President Bill Clinton. Instead of saying, "I did not have sexual relations with that woman," David fessed up to his sin (well, eventually). You see, it's one thing to be sorry for what you have done, and another for being truly repentant of the deeper sin within. I was always sorry for what I had done—I apologised ad nauseam to myself, God, or my wife. I was sorry on the surface purely out of fear of the consequences, of being found out some way, which I always tried so hard to avoid. I never took a step back and dug deep enough to weed out my tendency to relapse. An adulterous husband who has been caught and is sorry for hurting his wife isn't immune to returning to his sin. I've seen it time and time again: the tears, the apology, the asking of forgiveness, only to slip up again and again because they didn't truly immerse themselves in the mercy of God, looking at the deeper sin within and owning it.

Walking away from sin and leaving it for good requires a methodical action. I'm not proposing my own interpretation of the twelve-step program, merely nodding to the efficacy behind a systematic approach. There is a reason why it's called steps: there's a level of ascendancy and advancement in one's recovery. It's not just about hindsight and remorse. Feeling sorry isn't enough. So many men are constantly apologising, but you have to physically leave your sin in order to find redemption. You often hear guys say, 'Please, just give me a second chance.' It's a mistake that will foster further mistakes. It's not about second chances. I always asked for second chances, but it was never just one more—it was hundreds more. I was always changing and not terminating.

To leave sin behind the way King David did is to ameliorate and walk away from the self-reliant systems of your heart that cause you to sin in the first place. You need to distinguish between repentance and remorsefulness. The two are very different. Seeking recovery is non-negotiable if you are to be transformed. When I sought counsel, I wasn't immediately rehabilitated. I still had the propensity to relapse. I remember my counsellor saying to me that all the steps and programs and advice in the world are immaterial if the subject doesn't have the strong desire to change. When you make a choice to step out of your comfort zone and choose to create new, healthy habits, you create new neural networks. No one can create those new pathways but you. The onus is on you, and when you decide to change yourself, a new healthy habit is established.

Apart from counselling I also based a large part of my recovery on gamification, a word which was all the rage in Madison Avenue ad land not too long ago. Some might know it as a marketing technique to encourage engagement, like airline loyalty points; others might know it as the level-up you earned last night in *StarCraft*. I first came across this technique when I stole the title of "mayor" at my local Starbucks, thanks to the hey-day Foursquare app. I had certainly earned my title. Climbing the virtual ladder required dedication and, of course, copious amounts of grande caffè mochas. Eventually, I was usurped by an overeager upstart who seemed to be staking his claim along the high street. Nevertheless, I now prefer to make my own coffee, it's more rewarding. My attention has since changed course. Nowadays, I'm far more interested in receiving gold status with my preferred airline, so that I can maintain my level of perks. Be that as it may, there's a satisfaction in swiftly being ushered past the snakelike queues for check-in. This fascination for achieving gold status is nothing new. Gamification has also existed in millions of preschool classes around the world. Think back to your nursery school days, where the charts on the wall had everyone's name written down in crayon. Do you remember how next to every name was a hodgepodge placement of stars? If you were good enough to work your way through all the colours of the pack, you eventually received the coveted gold star. Even then, as four-year-olds, we were all rewarded for things we did correctly or, dare I say, habitually. It was gamification in analogue, but very effective. I haven't been immersed in the psychology of gamification, but I have seen the good in it. Removed from the marketing ploys and brand loyalty tricks, this science has helped me steer a more guided course, from a lustful life to a lust for life. In the past I tried and attended many programs and classes, but nothing seemed to stick. My attention and commitment petered out. Nothing seemed to work for me until I stumbled across a program while browsing in bed late one night. This program, based on gamification at its core, continues to help me work towards a daily practice of recovery. Just as a recovering alcoholic receives a sobriety coin for being sober for a certain amount of time, this program uses engaging rewards and points. It has managed to help me genuinely achieve a balance of psychology and entertainment.

Initially I was dubious. It appeared a frivolous gimmick for such a serious problem. On the contrary, it found the sweet spot, providing a relevant and genuine platform for today's tech-obsessed society. There's a wry yet ingenious irony in using the very same tools that fed my addiction for years as a platform for recovery. It's equally efficient on desktop and smartphone. Now help is with me wherever I go. Most importantly, it offers personal coaching and group meets. Instead of driving into the city after dark to meet in some cold, clinical, public hall for shortbread and tea, I can log on to a video call from wherever I happen to be. What's more, I have the option to meet in a similar age group or mixed. There's something for everyone.

Understandably, this might not be what you need. It certainly wasn't the silver bullet for me but it became a satisfactory substitute for logging into my group chat rather than sex chat. Like any recovery, help is there if you want it, but you have to be willing to put yourself out there by making that first step. One thing is certain, you won't find victory unless you're willing to lose your pride.

Redemption

There are three things you or your partner needs to recognise to overcome unwanted sexual behaviour. First, dig deep to find what is missing in life. What needs to be replaced and why? What is lacking? What emptiness is troubling you? Second, sin needs to be acknowledged for what it is. It shouldn't be caked in excuses, hidden behind, or used as a scapegoat. It must be called out, laid bare, and exposed to the light. Sin cannot survive without darkness. Third, there's a huge distinction between being remorseful and being repentant. They are not the same. It's not about being sorry for the conse-quences. It's about taking control and turning away from sin and towards God. Lastly, systematic thinking and planning must come to fruition for recovery to begin its work. Identify the issues and the tools needed to confi-dently walk away from what caused the sin in the first place. Then comes the task of reinterpreting everything your mind distorted, because it isn't just about stopping lustful tendencies but about recovering attraction and beauty as something consciously fixed towards the complete person. We always see giving up something as a negative. The most important thing for you to do is to look at what you will gain. It might feel like you're giving up an exciting, familiar habit, but, trust me, you'll be gaining far more. You'll realise you never lost anything, including yourself.

13

TOXICITY OF PLASTICITY

MY RELENTLESS CYCLE OF ADDICTION SEEMED insurmountable. I had given up all hope in foolishly thinking otherwise. I believed, as scientists once did, that the brain was incapable of further growth once it reached adulthood—all the stretching and augmenting slowed once my voice broke. Scientists used to believe the brain was hardwired at birth and that its ability to grow beyond childhood was only possible if a person suffered from a traumatic injury or severe illness that would shape and alter it to be different. This notion has since been disproved. We now know that the brain is the ultimate organ of adaptation. It changes and upgrades (not as painfully frequent as iOS), constantly rewiring, laying down new nerve connections. You might have heard the term *neuroplasticity*—the ability for your brain to reorganise itself, both physically and functionally, throughout your life due to your environment, behaviour, thinking, and emotions. Your brain can just as easily generate negative changes as positive ones. The more I understood about why I behaved the way I did, the way in which I responded to things, and how I could undo what I had previously learned, the more hope I felt.

The more I struggled with my own internal battles, the more I began educating myself on why I behaved a certain way and why my brain seemed to always respond to triggers the way it did. Getting better was always my goal, but understanding how my mind worked helped me approach my addiction in a constructive way. It showed me why I found it increasingly difficult to prevent my mind from falling for cheap fixes. The theory was as important as the practice. Some of you feel crippled at the moment, just as I was; but you can walk again, my friends. Not in a surreal, Benny-Hinn-convention kind of way, but through a mental and behavioural shift. You have the power to stretch and shape the way you think and act. You can change the way you think. As in other areas of life, the more you know and understand, the less you're left in the dark.

Sexual addiction never arrived one day to usurp my life like some Pacific tidal wave. I dipped my toe in the water, slowly moving further in until I was swept away by a strong current. My unwanted behaviour was formed over time until it became a 'natural' habit. It began with certain things triggering a desire and leading my thinking farther and farther along, until I found myself repeatedly acting on every impulse. Although I had no idea of how I arrived at the point I did, I soon learned to accept it as part of the norm. Now, it's important to note that there are two thought camps when it comes to sexual addiction, particularly on the subject of pornography. There are some who try to prove that it has harmful side effects, and then there are those who shrug it off as nothing more than a harmless fantasy—a natural, carnal proclivity. Like Mr Tank and condom wrapper girl. I would argue that as flighty as a fantasy might seem, it still has the ability to be harmful because it can so quickly transcend from the realm of a private affair to a public health issue (more on that later). No one ever died from opening a *Penthouse* centrefold, but the slow, internal death of the soul from habitual viewing will eventually sap the life from you. The harmful effects of pornography continue to divide, but the science of how your brain responds to it is irrefutable—this much we do know (remember the guy whose brain lit up like digital billboard?). Dr Judith Reisman, an American conservative academic and author, best known for her condemnation of sexologist Alfred Kinsey, exposed fraud in sex science and education. Some of you might be familiar with Kinsey's name if you've watched the 2004 biopic starring Liam Neeson. Ironically, it hit the silver screen the same year Dr Reisman gave a persuasive testimony before the U.S. Senate Committee on Commerce, Science, and Transportation. I would've paraphrased her findings, but I think that when it comes to studies it's important to capture the whole transcript. If anything, it'll give you a fascinating insight into the neurological insights of pornography on the brain:

Thanks to the latest advances in neuroscience, we now know that *emotionally arousing images imprint and alter the brain*, triggering an instant, involuntary, but lasting, *biochemical memory trail*.

This applies to so-called 'soft-core' and 'hard-core' pornography, which may, arguably, subvert the First Amendment by overriding the cognitive speech process.

Once our neurochemical pathways are established they are difficult or impossible to delete. Erotic images also commonly trigger the viewer's 'fight or flight' sex hormones producing *intense arousal states* that appear to fuse the conscious state of libidinous arousal with unconscious emotions of fear, shame, anger and hostility.

These media erotic fantasies become deeply imbedded, commonly coarsening, confusing, motivating and addicting many of those exposed. (See 'The Violence Pyramid' at http://www.vbii.org/violence.html).

Pornography triggers a myriad of endogenous, internal, natural drugs that mimic the 'high' from a street drug. Addiction to pornography is addiction to what I dub erototoxins—mind altering drugs produced by the viewer's own brain.

How does this 'brain sabotage' occur? Brain scientists tell us that "in 3/10 of a second a visual image passes from the eye through the brain, and whether or not one wants to, the brain is structurally changed and memories are created—we literally 'grow new brain' with each visual experience."[1]

In advertising, there's a saying: understand the why, and you'll find the solution to the problem. Only after reading Reisman's testimony did my understanding of what I was experiencing make sense. My brain had changed. Years of feeding my brain with all kinds of provocative imagery had definitely produced a noticeable structural and behavioural change in me. I found that during intimate moments with my wife, my brain would somehow hijack my attention, causing my body to react differently, making me unable to perform. As Reisman puts it, a 'brain sabotage' eventually left me (brain) damaged. Years of viewing unrealistic, manipulated imagery didn't make me empowered as a man—it left me humiliated.

Still, my wife sympathised. She wasn't happy about

my condition, but she understood the reason. I openly
discussed how years of conditioning impacted the way
I reciprocated love and that if I was to work on changing, it would require "reformatting my brain". I would
essentially be starting over again with a new, reconditioned brain. It sounds very Shelley's Frankenstein, but
it's nothing monstrous. Essentially it meant I would
have to unlearn all the misleading lies I had fed my
brain and relearn true beauty. Only then would I see my
wife for who she is rather than who I assume she
should be. What should've been a healthy sexual relationship within marriage was not, and my appetite for
sex drastically waned. Growing up, no one thinks of
the damage they might be doing to themselves. I never
considered the possibility of trauma let alone the word.
I had zero knowledge about the adverse effects that
years of conditioning would have on me. I certainly
didn't think about the impact it would have on my
future wife. I stubbornly believed that my actions were
harmless—a lie I was fed in the media time and time
again: 'Relax, it's natural . . . . It's what guys do . . . .
There's no evidence to suggest it's harmful . . . . It's a
little bit of naughty fun.' Yet, while the media spouts
flippant rhetoric, people's lives and relationships are
falling apart. The worst defence I often hear is, "Oh,
but not everyone is affected by it." That's right, they're
not. Not everyone becomes a sexual monster. Just like
you don't automatically become an alcoholic if you
drink a beer. A friend I knew who would have a beer

after work every day, never going over the limit, and found out years later during a random trip to the doctor that his liver had deteriorated badly. Sometimes the side-effects are slow-burning and might not be as rampant and savage as addiction suggests.

I remember years ago watching a TV documentary about the notorious serial killer Ted Bundy. It was an interview on death row an hour before he was to be executed. The interviewer was American evangelical author James Dobson, and he asked a question that I'll never forget. About midway into the interview, Dobson asked Bundy to elaborate on the antecedents of his behaviour, which many would deem grotesque. Dobson kept prodding to find the turning point of Bundy's behaviour. With nothing left to lose, his response was as clinical and lifeless as the room itself. In some small glimmer of redemption, he began with repudiating any admission of playing the victim, yet he strongly acknowledged certain contributing factors that influenced his behaviour. Before elaborating any further, he prefaced by recounting his childhood growing up in a loving Christian home, in a house void of any adolescent misgivings. Like any young boy, he would often explore the surrounding neighbourhoods and alleyways. An innocent curiosity led him to a discovery of adult magazines in another person's trash. Pair this with the odd, dark, detective magazines, and you have an unhealthy recipe for ruminating all kinds of thoughts. But according to Bundy, it was never the sole reason leading him to act out maliciously the way he did years later. However, it did have an influence over him which amassed over time. One thing led to another. He confessed, 'It doesn't make you a serial killer, but it does have a damaging effect on you.'

In Bundy's case, pornography nudged the pendulum to a very dark and violent side. Others might not sway as violently, but their behaviour might still be affected in more obscure ways. I never imagined how such an influence could distort my own friendships, romantic relationships, family, work, and passions. But I wasn't blindsided either. I had a self-awareness that something was amiss; it wasn't enough to snap me out of it, but thankfully it was enough to stop me from going to any extremes. Wisdom is something that you bring to your life—it comes from awareness and experience.

I often wonder how much more someone like Bundy would've been affected had he had easy access to mobile devices and the internet. It concerns me when I think about the adverse effects to which today's generation is exposed. Writer Belinda Luscombe aptly points out in her thought-provoking *Time* article 'Porn and the Threat to Virility':

A growing number of young men are convinced

their sexual responses have been sabotaged because their brains were virtually marinated in porn when they were adolescents. Their generation has consumed explicit content in quantities and varieties never before possible, on devices designed to deliver content swiftly and privately, all at an age when their brains were more plastic — more prone to permanent change — than in later life. These young men feel like unwitting guinea pigs in a largely unmonitored decade-long experiment in sexual conditioning.[2]

If our brain is a sponge, and our memory a fridge full of marinated imagery, eventually a discerning taste will be impossible to distinguish. The more filth I fed my brain, the more distorted my palate became. True beauty was substituted by artificial sweeteners. I was lucky enough not to grow up with the internet. I say lucky because I'm grateful for my youth spent just being a boy running around a garden, not servant to the TV. Access to any kind of explicit imagery was never immediate or on a whim. It had to be a carefully planned operation just to get hold of a 'girly' magazine from the local corner newsagent. I had a better chance of buying a pack of B&H Special Milds over the counter. So I did both hoping that it appeared normal. I personally never had any access to videotapes of such a persuasion unless a friend had discovered his dad's secret VHS collection by chance. The only supply channel to higher-grade material was in who you knew and the different tricks you'd pick up from the more seasoned kids at school. One friend in particular hid his porn by bookending them between a blockbuster movie he copied onto VHS. So when he handed out movies like Jaws and Rambo, it appeared perfectly normal. His collection of Hollywood movies on his bedroom shelf certainly didn't seem out of place to his parents.

Back then there was a much bigger mystery to it all, which at times made the allure and fascination greater than the need to fuel a sexual hunger. Nowadays any sudden urge can be fed within seconds. You never really have time to wrestle with your addiction or the temptation to counteract it. I can only imagine how difficult it must be for young men growing up with unadulterated access and how they'll be once they reach marriage—if they ever get there.

As Luscombe's article mentions, more and more young men are having less sex because of an abundance of pornographic material. Mutual consent in a healthy relationship has become less appealing than ease of access. Human responses like feelings, intimacy, and mood have very little relevance anymore. In such a small amount of time, it has gotten even worse because of the increasing pace of technological advancement. The scary facts point to the past decade of demise. Digital access to pornography became an exponentially pervasive component in our lives. In 2007, broadband internet reached 50 per cent of Americans—the same year the ubiquitous Pornhub was founded, and two years following the launch of YouTube.[3]

To give a bit of perspective on how disconcerting it was back then, there were 58 million monthly U.S. visitors to adult sites out of a total of 167 million U.S. internet users.[4] When we jump to 2013, the stats are similar but contextual to the advancement of technology. American smartphone ownership exceeded 50 percent of the nation's population.[5] The significant jump wasn't in the innovative prowess, but that over six years society went from having free access to porn to having free access to porn anytime, anyhow, anywhere. This closed the age gap dramatically. Even more alarming, the average age of young men who now view porn is between eleven and thirteen years old. They most likely make up the twelve million hours a day spent viewing porn globally on Pornhub.[6] The cold, hard reality is that by the time these young boys reach their twenty-first birthday, they will have been knee-deep in viewing porn for nearly a decade. Worse, probably everything they've learned about sex will have come from the adult footage they were seeing and sharing. 10 long years of shaping their mind. Now imagine starting a serious relationship after having spent years invested in content that is anything but monogamous and loving.

I've always found the irony in pornographic statistics, as I'm convinced of the increasing difficulty in finding any control group willing and honest enough to conduct any conclusive studies. In any test, you need two or more subjects to compare, and finding teenage boys today who have never looked at porn before, or who don't look at it currently, is almost impossible. As Professor Simon Louis Lajeunesse, of Montreal University in Canada suggests, 'We started our research seeking men in their twenties who had never consumed pornography. We couldn't find any.'[7]

If you know how the brain works, it's a lot easier to understand why you or someone close to you is acting out the way they are. When I explained to my wife how the rewards centre of the brain worked, she had a better understanding of why I would so easily lose control. It's not enough to tell your partner that, 'men as the collective whole' are visual creatures. It's just a stupid cop-out as far as I'm concerned. If you have eyes, you're visual; women are visual, too, so I don't completely buy this notion. However, I do believe that men have been conditioned visually far more as young boys than girls have. The rewards circuit over thousands of years has developed to respond to natural rewards—things we need to sustain our daily lives, whether it's finding food, eating, intercourse, or being in communal relationships. These have always been core to our living environment. Over time this started to change when man introduced 'extreme' rewards, beyond what is sufficient. These new extreme rewards would cause the dopamine in our brain to overflow. I imagine it must've been an intense feeling. Any form of pleasure to our brain is acknowledged as something good for us. Extreme rewards can lead to bingeing, whether on a Big Mac or a slab of Dairy Milk. You're getting it while the getting's good, so munch until your heart's content.

Biology professor Gary Wilson explains how all of this works.[8] A surge in dopamine basically flicks a molecular switch in our brain called Delta FosB, which sounds like some sort of SEAL ops team about to drop in through a roof. Every time there's a spike in excitement, it causes your dopamine to surge, which then kicks in the Delta FosB, and it accumulates over time (think of it being stored up like an arsenal). This excess Delta FosB has the ability to alter the brain, and, by doing so, it stimulates a habitual cycle of craving or overindulgence. The more this Delta FosB builds up, the more the bingeing accumulates, to the point where the brain changes. For the sake of analogy, imagine someone toying with soft drugs at a party. Over time you notice them doing it more and more, at any chance they can. The brain adapts to the craving of the high, and the effects are less powerful than they were the first few times at the party. So what does the brain do? Well, it craves the initial high, which means there's a propensity to seek out harder drugs.

In other words, Professor Wilson is saying that with things like online porn, the constant novelty of the click can gradually create addictive traits. As soon as a young boy makes his first click, the everyday pleasures considered to be normal in society eventually become unsatisfying for him. His receptive brain has become hyperreactive to the provocative imagery he is viewing. As his frontal cortex changes over time, so too does his willpower—it gets weaker and weaker, eroding within. Sometimes I think it's easier to sympathise with a drug addict because I perceive their battle as a chemical response, assuming it to be unmanageable and therefore playing them more as a victim than a culprit. It's easier to wrap your head around why someone is desperate to shoot up or find the next fix. You believe to some degree that their body has wrestled with their mind and won; therefore, they must have little control over their actions. Sure, you'll still be repulsed or saddened by the addiction, but you're under no illusion that the chemicals won't have a massive influence over reason.

Sadly, the reverse is often true for sexual addiction. I suppose most people don't view it as a chemical issue, as in a solid or liquid substance overpowering your brain, but rather as more of a psychological condition. For most, a chemical connection is far more tenuous. So when a wife tells her husband to stop looking at other women, it shouldn't appear out of the ordinary for her to do so. It's a natural and obvious response

—"Stop! Close the laptop and get over it!" Like a parent telling her misbehaving child to stop annoying the family dog. Somehow I doubt anyone would expect a drug addict to crave less easily or not at all. Most people have a grasp of the complexities involved in such an addiction.

Once I understood how the brain worked, it helped me to understand my behaviour and explained why I struggled with my libido despite having a normal, healthy, sexual marriage. It notably waned after a couple of years of being married. In fact, I was worried. I couldn't explain it at the time, but after having read a lot of information, I realised I was suffering from erectile dysfunction, which was more of a surprise for me than the warning sign of a compromised relationship. In truth, my brain had been numbed from all the visual stimulation I was ingesting, so weaker signals were being sent to the parts of my body that I naturally expected to display healthy signs of arousal. It wasn't inherently a psychological issue, which is what I initially believed it to be. It was also physiological. My brain had in fact reconditioned itself. All the years of feeding my mind all kinds of unwarranted imagery had shaped the way I thought and responded. What's worse, I had become accustomed to sexual imagery playing a large part in triggering my pleasure points at times when I was so desperate to perform my role as a husband. I often had to conjure past imagery in my mind so that I could physically be up to the task. Messed up, right? I was relying on what my mind knew—an addiction to pixels. Instead of being present in a real moment, I was robbed and dragged away to something unrealistic. It might have been a temporary solution, but it left a permanent feeling of shame and guilt. It seems so obvious now, but had I only removed easy access to adult content, I would've been on the road to recovery. When you're in the thick of it, one single variable seems so insurmountable.

There are times when I'm scared of how much I already know, how much I have seen, and how much time I have invested in feeding my mind all kinds of unhealthy thoughts. I'm even surprised at my ability to have any inkling of clarity. I wasn't naive about the probability of the side effects. Just recently I came across an article that highlighted a report by the Royal Society for Public Health in the UK.[9] It addressed how amongst all the social networks, Instagram appears to have the greatest negative effects on mental health. I'm not surprised. As a predominantly visual platform with over 700 million users and more than 40 billion photos shared to date, it's no wonder that it contributes heavily to feelings of anxiety, depression, sleep deprivation, sexual addiction, body-image issues, and who knows what else. I found myself aimlessly flicking through my social feeds first thing in the morning and just before bed. I now leave my phone outside the bedroom. These social networks are designed to serve you every minute of the day, wherever you are. We even have a name for this: social feed. Think about it: it feeds you constantly so that your attention isn't diverted elsewhere. And this information is supplied to you at a rapid rate where habits are formed instantly. It's a deeply concerning reality and one that makes it harder to avoid. With an influx of imagery all around me, I was never under the illusion that full recovery was an easy road. An alcoholic can change the route he takes every day to avoid the pub, but it's harder to detour when your brain has a bank of provocative imagery saved and on repeat. I knew defeating my Goliath would require grit and smarts. You have to be resolute in making those images slowly fade. Even now I can still recall images and thoughts I experienced as a horny school kid. I don't want to recall them, but I'm aware of the few remnants I still carry around with me to this day. It doesn't mean I am still a slave to them, but I have found life hacks that help substitute my thoughts with positive imagery and experiences while eventually pushing away any unwarranted ones.

I am very aware of what I have seen and can remember, and I have talked about it and prayed about it often, pleading with God to renew my mind and make it clean. But I must also play a part in intentionally choosing what experiences I now allow to enter my mind. If something grabs you with enough passion and attention in a way that's positive and constructive, you're more than likely strong enough to wean yourself away from any addiction without having to overthink it.

Knowledge

It's natural to feel like your partner's addiction is immediately your fault. It's not. I have had to work through these very issues with my wife, reassuring her that she bears no responsibility for my actions. It all falls on me. Regardless, it never makes for a comfortable conversation. For the most part, it has been tough, but I've been determined to be up front in assuring her that the heavy load rests on me. It's hard to sound convincing when you have compromised trust, and part of the process is to educate rather than convince the other affected party. When I slowly showed her how the brain works and how specific actions I am struggling with can bring about erectile dysfunction, it didn't absolve me of any guilt or prop me up as some victim, but it allowed her to understand the gravity of my uncontrollable addiction. I first acknowledged my actions as my responsibility. Second, if we were to have a healthy, loving marriage moving forward, it was up to me to reshape my mind for the better. She understood that a change in our marriage would flourish only if we both realised the why and how.

It helped provide a platform to build on the work that needed doing. As soon as my wife stopped blaming herself and supported me and gave me time and space to reboot and recondition my brain, it made the journey together a lot easier. Something that had tried to separate us for years ended up bringing us together in a healthy, new way.

14

DOES YOUR STORY REPEAT ITSELF?

THE FIRST RESPONSE ALWAYS GIVEN WHEN SOMETHING terrible happens to someone is: Why? Why me? Why now? Why not him or her? Why on earth? Why, why, why? Once the emotions have simmered, the follow-up question to the first usually starts with: How? How will I move forward? How do I overcome this? How do I get out of this jar of pickles? How can this get any better? How, how, how? The problem with the latter set of questions is that you haven't first understood and addressed *why*. Only then will you be able to answer *how*. Ask any entrepreneur to name the main ingredient to their success, and they'll unequivocally echo the word 'why.' It's the one word that propelled them on their trajectory. Why book a cab using Uber? Why type on a MacBook? Why slip past the McDonald's drive-thru on your way home? Why listen to music streaming apps? All these questions started with 'why' before anyone figured out how such a dream could become a reality.

It's impossible to count how many times I've asked 'why' without ever investigating all the avenues of my unwanted behaviour. Instead, I've impatiently jumped straight to 'how.' I would eat up all the tangible and practical solutions I could find with the promise of finding everlasting freedom. I'd sign up for courses, online tutorials, virtual accountability partners, apps, retreats, bots, and software programs in the hope of finally 'kicking it.' Initially, the signs of progress were promising, but this would only ever last a few weeks, possibly a month if I was lucky. The recovery programs all had their merit; however, when put into practice in isolation, they were nothing more than temporary obstacles. Sanctions of the senses are a diversion, not a solution. 'How' and 'why' must work together harmoniously to address the heart of the issue.

In the advertising industry, it's impossible to produce brilliant creative work for brands without a sound strategy. A strategist's role requires the ability to delve deep inside the brand, mining and panning as much useful information as possible until they unearth any nuggets. These nuggets are invaluable to the creative process and are delivered in the form of a brief to be interpreted by a creative team. Without them, a brand has very little to say. Usually when this happens, the advertising resorts to shouting at you in starbursts, flashing and slashing prices. Beating you over the head is anything but memorable. It's annoying wallpaper. The nuggets are commonly referred to as 'insights,' from which a brand proposition is written. A proposition or value statement is what sets any brand apart. It's giving consumers a reason to believe why they should choose you over anyone else. Knowing these insights helps the creatives brainstorm clever ways to bring a campaign to life. They'll often demonstrate how your life will become even richer if you had (insert brand name here).

A couple of years back there was a successful campaign I loved out of Australia called 'Melanoma Likes Me.' The advertising agency created a simple campaign using a unique algorithm that found and responded to popular hashtags on Instagram relating to all things Aussie summer and that geolocated images with a like and response from @_melanoma. This was a clever brand response that didn't require a big-budget commercial. It only ever appeared on Instagram.

Allow me to take a step back and walk you through the process. Australia has one of the highest rates of skin cancer in the world, two to three times the rates in Canada, the United States, and the United Kingdom. What's even more eye-opening is that general practitioners have over one million patient consultations per year for skin cancer alone.[1] What we know is that

Aussies worldwide are renowned for being avid sun worshippers. The sun, beach, and surfing go hand in hand—"They just can't get a bloody 'nuff of it, mate." These fun-in-the-sun adventure snaps are usually punctuated with #sunsoutgunsout #summer #bondi #beachday, or whatever hashtag leaves you feeling jealous and suffering a severe amount of #fomo. Once the strategists find these insights, they can then align them with the brand's proposition—something like 'Whenever you're in the sun, so is melanoma.' The creative solution almost wrote itself. Every time someone shared their snaps, they got a like from a new friend, @_melanoma, and also sometimes a cheeky reply to their posts, like: 'Perfect weather for me too! #killerweather.' When people clicked on the handle, it would open an in-app experience providing useful information and tips on how to check for melanomas. This campaign is smart because it first understands the consumer behaviour and then talks directly to the environment in which they are engaging, in this case Instagram. Without a great insight, a typical and boring campaign would've been created instead. The insight (WHY) paved a way forward for a solution (HOW).

If you've ever visited a clinical psychologist or counsellor, you'll automatically begin by addressing your current matters, but a psychologist will always start by pulling you back to your childhood. It can feel invasive at times, but the past, not the present, is where the answers lie. Restoration doesn't begin where you currently are; it starts with unravelling your past so you can rebuild your future.

I've always believed my addiction had nothing to do with my childhood. Well, of course, it did in an autobiographical sense, because, like most adolescents, I was introduced to nudity, porn, and all things alluring at that time. My response to this unwanted sexual behaviour was often child-like and automated—never something I gave much thought to. My story didn't feel any different from that of my peers. To my limited understanding, I believed we all shared a common biological response that followed a predetermined script. You become curious about your body. A friend introduces you to nudity. And you begin to experience chemical reactions inside of you that are completely foreign. This exploration carries on through your late teens. The more you discover, the more curious you become, and this continually perks your interest. Formats change with technological advancement, and you become even more incapable of dealing with the sensory overload. All the while, in the back of your mind, you're convinced these boyish habits of yours will inevitably disappear once you're in a healthy, committed sexual relationship. And then one day you arrive at the end of the script only to realise your story is open for adaptation. So you add a monologue to the script, assuring yourself that it's all natural and that your body is reacting how it's biologically intended to. But you realise something's missing, so you decide to throw in more money and special effects to keep the new scenes entertaining. You feel like Michael Bay, and before you know it you've lost the plot.

For a long time it never dawned on me that my past is a roadmap to my addiction. And the reason I never gave it much thought was because I never felt like I had suffered any trauma. In my script, there was no Shakespearean tragedy or drama. I was never sexually abused, my parents didn't divorce, I didn't grow up poor, there was no weird, dodgy uncle. I had more love from my parents than any child could ever hope for. Christian values weren't foreign to me; they were the bricks of our home life, assembled on a foundation that was God-centred. When there's trauma, the dots are easier to connect, and the diagnosis is precise. My situation was murky and required a hard look. Without going into the specifics, my childhood was peppered with road signs. There was rife adultery in our church and serial infidelity from the pastor; guilt and shame were common themes, and premarital sex was the target of fire and brimstone so often preached from the pulpit. 1. *Sex equalled fear*. At home, sex wasn't an open, insightful, educational conversation. It was awkward, mostly consisting of my mother hammering in the mantra of abstaining every thought and desire till marriage. Any curious exploration before marriage is a sin. So get on your bike, ride around the block, and pray and pedal till you exhaust yourself (true story). 2. *Sex equalled anxiety.* You can start to see the unhealthy cracks and two pervasive themes. Couple them with confidence issues and unhealthy friendships at school, and my present state of mind offers a clearer explanation as to why.

I don't believe I am a victim of unwanted sexual behaviour, but when I look back on my past, the hovering effects played a role in my vulnerability to unhealthy sexual curiosity. Jay Stringer, a mental health counsellor, believes our sexual fantasies and behaviour are not as random as we're led to believe. In an enlightening article called 'What Your Sexual Fantasies (Might) Say About You,' he addresses quantifiable findings conducted from research with over 3,600 men and women on critical drivers of unwanted sexual behaviour: pornography, affairs, paid-for sex, etcetera.

What I can tell you is that sexual struggles are not random or capricious. They develop in the formative emotional and sexual soil of your childhood and flourish in the unaddressed dynamics of your present life. My research found that the type of pornography and sexual behavior you pursue can be predicted by the major themes and significant relationships that have marked your life.

One of the most common sexual fantasies for men had to do with the desire for power over women. Other popular fantasies for men included: a desire for women to have power over them, a diverse choice in sexual partners, sex that was aggressive or violent, an affair, and buying sex. Men who wanted power over women tended to pursue pornography where women were younger, had a smaller body type, and had a particular race or appearance that suggested (to them) subservience. What predicted this type of sexual fantasy in men? There are three key drivers: (1) His level of shame (2) His sense of futility (3) Growing up with a strict father. Men with the highest levels of shame were those that wanted the most power over women. The writing on the wall is that men find power over women arousing precisely because it gives them an arena to find dominance amidst a life filled with shame and futility.

While some men found having power over women arousing, others in my research tended to want the woman in pornography to have the power. These men often fantasised about older women, attractive mother figures, or women in positions of authority who would pursue them. What were the key predictors for this type of sexual fantasy? (1) A man's depression (2) A history of sexual abuse (3) A father who confided in his son about his personal life and marriage difficulties. Once you dive deeper into the 'why' of your sexual fantasies, you quickly enter the stories that await your engagement.[2]

Stringer's research reassured me that sexual fantasies are not the result of repugnant behaviour but in fact are a biographical wayfinder inviting us to a journey of understanding, healing, and transformation. Recounting and reliving my past wasn't something that happened on a quiet Sunday afternoon. It took months of deep personal reflection to locate and isolate my common themes and traumas. I often struggled to remember things. I would write what I could recall, and then, just like a true detective who'd link the evidence to a location with a red thread on a corkboard, I'd draw a line from a sentence and connect it to familiar behavioural patterns or fantasies. It wasn't always immediately obvious, but I would write key observations down anyway and then try to unpack it a few days later. Sometimes something seemingly subtle or trivial was often overlooked, and later I would find the elusive missing piece in the puzzle and finally begin to see something taking shape. Talking through these observations with a counsellor, close friend, or partner also helped to slowly massage some of the guilt and shame away. On date nights with my wife, it helped to talk through things with her about what I had done or noticed in my childhood. Just verbalising my thoughts allowed me to process and decode a lot of the information floating around inside my brain. Understanding that my past manifested a lot of unwanted behaviour in the present made it easier to constructively address any recurring patterns instead of repressively ignoring them. The more questions you begin to ask, whether scientific, spiritual, biological, behavioural, or biographical, the more you'll open your mind to knowledge and understanding as to *why*. And this will make the road to *how* less narrow to tread.

Healing

Guilt, shame, futility, and anger are transposed when you recognise your behaviour, take ownership, and open yourself completely to a journey of pursuing truth and understanding. If you repress the pain and confusion from your childhood, it will be destined to manifest itself. Not dealing with it will mean others will have to. Someone who grows up in a house of anger is likely to become an angry person. Being a parent, I am fully conscious that every action and word out of my mouth has the potential to be observed and mimicked by my child. My actions are transferable. Having insight into your life will help you find the nuggets you need to find how to overcome your addiction. Take time out to write a journal of scenarios, scenes, or instances you feel had an effect on you. It might not be something significant or obvious, but jot it down anyway. Then think about how old you were when you started being sexually curious.

How did your behaviour change? Then look at your current situation—your triggers and sexual fantasies. Are they always the same? Is there a common thread? Then together with a friend, counsellor, or partner, someone with whom you feel you can be honest, try to piece your past with your unwanted behaviour. Once you understand why you behave and act out the way you do, you'll realise how you got there—but, more importantly, how you can leave.

15

MIGHT I PROPOSE A PURPOSE?

Addiction is the enemy of true purpose.

— ANONYMOUS

I HAD FINALLY MADE IT TO THE FORMIDABLE FURBER Steps, in the Blue Mountains—a hard reality check reminding me there was one kilometre left to go. At a rough ascent of 221 m and a total elevation of 942 m, the steps (all 951 of them, to be precise) were originally hand-carved with a hammer and chisel in 1908 by Thomas Furber, a land surveyor. I was hobbling on the forty-ninth kilometre of the North Face 50 km Ultra Trail Australia, so the sheer thought of heading directly vertical meant that my legs would have to endure further punishment. My quads were completely blown, but I knew there wasn't any alternative; the steps were narrow, and with runners following me there was nowhere to go but up. I regrettably didn't have my trekking poles, so hunching forward and placing my hands on my knees was the only additional support to propel my body forward. Every step was a gasp for air. The faint noise of the crowd and the clanging tin of the cowbells signalled me home like some lost sheep. Although I hadn't run a particularly good race, I wasn't fazed. My measure of success was never against the clock, only the finish line. At the start I kept remembering to pace myself, telling my body to conserve as much energy early on as I could. If I could keep a consistent pace, then the rest of my body would surely take care of itself.

Five kilometres in, the wheels started to come off, and I knew it would take a lot more than just physical strength to get through the remaining forty-five. Two weeks before the race the warning signs were there. After what would be my last big training run before tapering, I started to feel a sharp pain along the right side of my shin, just under my knee cap. It felt like someone was poking a broken branch against the side of my knee. At first I thought nothing of the pain. I assumed that a couple of stretches and a hot bath should do the trick, but when the niggle persisted I booked one last trip to the physiotherapist in the hope of tweaking it out. It turns out what I thought to be a niggle was ITB syndrome.

If you're a runner, you'll be familiar with the acronym. It's a common overuse injury among runners, especially those who practice long-distance running. The iliotibial band is a thick band of fascia attached to the knee and is crucial for stabilising the knee while running, as it moves from behind the femur to the front of the femur during activity. The severe pain I experienced meant that the ITB band was not working as well as it should. When this is the case, most runners are sidelined for weeks, if not longer. I knew that a huge part of this injury was because I didn't stretch as well as I should've during my prior weeks of training. I wasn't disciplined with strength training either. I love getting out and putting in the kilometres, but I loathe the finicky pre- and post-run bits you're supposed to do. I paid the price on race day, and since then I've learned my lesson: don't ever skip your stretches. My stubbornness had caught up with me early on, but I was determined to finish, even if it meant I walked the whole way.

Seeing my wife at the first aid station lifted my spirits better than the flavoured electrolytes on offer. It helped me get through the next stage of the race, where every metre of decline sent a sharp pain jolting through my body. I wish I could go back and listen to the conversations I was having with myself. It was a rapid fire of 'Should I, shouldn't I?' Part of me just wanted to chuck it all in. The probability of running with unbearable pain for 45 km seemed absurd. Even my physio warned me to pull out if the pain became

any more severe, to avoid even more damage to my
leg. I remembered all the effort I had put in and the
months of training leading up to this—all the weekends I would spend carving the trails in the mountains instead of going out for Instagram-filtered
breakfasts with friends. This wasn't a pride thing, it
was about a determination to see something through.
So I pushed on. I don't remember how, I just did. I
found something deep within myself and felt new
again.

I remember a similar experience when I was riding a
100 km cycle race and seeing a guy next to me without
a seat. Only a seatpost. We were already 30 km in. I
don't know if he lost it or if he wanted to be the butt of
a joke, but he somehow found a way to finish unseated.
So for the rest of the trail run, I ran in a metronomic
trance, my feet hitting the dirt at the right beats as I
weaved my way along the canyon floor dressed under
heavy, crisp, green foliage. Strangely, looking back on
the race data on my GPS watch, I ran the fastest I had
run the whole day during the last 10 to 15 km, at my
most tired state. I recall passing people, but I don't
completely understand how I was strong enough to do
so or what triggered me to step on the gas. Having
started in the light, I finished in the dark. My time was
irrelevant, but all the clichés used to describe crossing

the line are true. I get it now. I have done races in the past but nothing even comparatively as tough as this.

I began trail running not because I wanted to fill a trophy cabinet, beat a time, make a podium finish, or turn pro. As great as all those achievements are, it's not why I took to the trails in the first place. I only started because it gave me a reason to get out of the house on the weekends and explore the countryside. Whenever I had any downtime I would seek out a new route and hit the trails. There's something quite magical about running on trails as opposed to roads. The enjoyment of jumping from rock to rock, hopping over tree roots, and springing through the forest reminded me of when I was a kid—how I used to explore for hours outside, sans my mother screaming for me to return for dinner. It also offers a great overall body workout that I find less demanding on the knees compared to pounding the tarmac.

Besides the physical and psychological benefits, there's also the spiritual. Some people go to the gym, paint, swim, hike, walk their dog, or do yoga to switch off and meditate. For me it's the trails. I don't meditate in an ethereal kind of way. It's more a chance for me to escape the bustling city to be quiet and just be— hearing my breath, slowing down my heart, and listening to my body. Most of the time I don't think about anything. Something so simple is incredibly cathartic. The forward motion and the quick-footed navigation often don't allow my mind to be bombarded with thoughts. I love it because I struggle to be silent when still. But it's not all airy-fairy tiptoeing. It can be hard work, particularly when training for a race. In that instance I can be out for five hours or more at a time.

Trail running isn't just a passion of mine—it's a lifesaver. All the additional gains above are peripheral. The biggest win is how it has helped me centre myself and deal with my addiction. If it weren't for running, I honestly believe that I'd be completely helpless. There's no exaggeration in how it has helped me focus and be better disciplined. Without discipline, I wouldn't achieve anything. I'd be hard pressed in trying to reach or achieve any goals I set. If I hadn't found a love for running and stuck at it, I probably wouldn't have gotten up at 4 a.m. every day to write this book before I went to work. It taught me that I can overcome any resistance through dogged persistence.

With any addiction, the greatest crime of all is its propensity to rob your productivity and steal time in ways you would never imagine. Everything you dream of doing is often sidelined before you can do anything about it. Then one day you look back and wonder how you wasted your time. Running, particularly trail running, has helped me to focus my attention away from everyday distractions. It has given me a space to shut out the noise, as well as incremental goals to work towards. The fitter I have gotten, the more it has helped me reclaim a portion of my brain. Every metre gained is a war of attrition. I might not have claimed every inch of my thoughts, but it has provided me with strategic insight into a better path.

The other thing trail running has done for me, and it's probably the biggest reason I do it, is that it has forced me to physically distance myself from susceptible environments. I leave the house when a gracious amount of time has been gifted to me. I usually hit the trails quite early. I find that running in first light is cooler and that there's less chance of crossing paths with a snake. Most importantly, it helps me to start my day with positive intent. I'd say I'm meticulous in setting a benchmark for how I want my day to flow. I know that if I'm disciplined enough, I'll be more in control of the rest of my day. Some like to run in groups, others prefer club meet-ups. I prefer the solitude because I don't get distracted by tit-for-tat competitiveness with other runners. A lot of my friends have asked if I get lonely running in a forest for so many hours. As an introvert, I naturally cherish the idea of being away from it all, on my own in nature. But whatever the environment, I don't find being around myself as difficult as it might be for some. I feed off it; it's how my soul recharges.

I'm also heightened to the fact that as much as I love any alone time, isolation isn't conducive to a life of recovery. It can be counterintuitive. Running on a trail isn't quite the same as being home alone with everything disposable at your fingertips. Whatever your addiction, too much time on your hands is a signal to your brain to spark the dopamine neurotransmitters in your frontal lobes. I know that when my wife is out and I'm left to my own devices, I'm at my most vulnerable, so I have to be particularly on guard. I'm never far from temptation. Nothing has changed since I was a teenager and my parents would go out for the evening, leaving me at home on my own. The only difference is that my brain learned to recognise a situation and trigger a response quicker. I've gotten a bit savvier since then and have slowly tried to train myself to counteract the sudden stampede of dopamine by avoiding an environment or changing course sooner. Trail running has given me a reason to discover more, physically and mentally. It has also helped me to set goals and work towards achieving them.

When I set out to run the North Face 50k, my wife was naturally supportive but understandably sceptical. This was my first running race, period. So when I set this ambitious goal and eventually achieved it, the reward wasn't only about finishing; it was about everything that led up to the starting line. The preparation for me was the rebuilding phase. The day of the race was my time to reflect and apply the training. As I ran the race, I felt I was living out the fruition of my hard labour: the months of grinding away, racking up the miles while I slogged through this newfound pain. There was something more in the accompaniment of finishing my training than in finishing the actual race. When I finally crossed the line I was emotional. It had meant a lot to finally get to the end, but even more so knowing I had completed something I had worked so hard towards. It was a different kind of special. I naturally gained so much later on than I gave on race day.

For starters, it helped set me up for applying a structure to any future goals. Running had provided me with an application for life and showed me what I could achieve when I used my time wisely. I had wasted so much of it in the past and felt completely crippled, but now I learned the practicality of slowly moving one leg in front of the other. Mental rehabilitation would require consistency. Every bit of momentum that inched me forward was an opportunity to reprogram my brain. The only way I could escape the fog in my mind was not to fritter away my free time. I'm not naive about the running clichés and metaphors. Everybody talks about the race of life: the winning and losing, crossing the metaphorical finish line. As cheesy as they are, the hard, cold fact is that achieving goals requires persistence, consistency, discipline, and determination—a lot like running.

I suppose the idea of using running to overcome an obstacle was an unavoidable metaphor in itself, but more a coincidental one. My ability to use running as a way to rebuild my life is by no means a prescriptive activity. I just happened to stumble into it, and it became a source and tool for recovery. It was a way to combat the negative aspects of my life. A substitute. As

Japanese author Haruki Murakami says in his book *What I Talk about When I Talk about Running*:

> 'To deal with something unhealthy, a person needs to be as healthy as possible . . . an unhealthy soul requires a healthy body.'[1]

Every time I hit the trails, I work up a sweat, running hard enough to release any soul-destroying toxins deep within me and paying for my transgressions one hill at a time. It wasn't so much a penance as a rite of passage. I enjoyed the sensation of feeling my body and mind dig deep to stay on course and I was adamant to reach my goal at any cost. This process produced a sense of mental clarity, coupled with a surge of physical energy. The two seemed to collaborate together quite nicely. When I began to restore those components, I experienced a metamorphosis that felt as if I had hit the reboot button. The more kilometres I ran, the more I shed some of my old skin, like a cowboy reeling at the prospect of removing his union suit after a long day on horseback. When I eventually crossed the finish line under the cold, crisp, May night sky, it proved to me the power of possibility.

As humans, we're naturally designed to work towards something. We need a reason to get up in the morning. Having a purpose and seeing your goals through to the end is not only rewarding but fundamentally character-building. Character-building represents progress. If you're not growing and developing in life, you cannot have the strength to pull yourself out of any unforeseeable situations in the future. When you're idle, your muscles are relaxed, you're weak, and it's impossible to stand up against anything thrown at you. But when you're moving, your muscles are developing as they grow stronger, adapting to any jut or obstacle that might break your momentum.

Not everybody wants to slip into a pair of running shoes and collect miles. Some of my friends would rather work their way through a series on Netflix than pound the tarmac after work. I get it, though I would argue that if you're looking to be free from an addiction, having something healthy to focus your mind and time on is crucial. It doesn't have to be running (or any form of physical exercise), but it should be a routine activity that will benefit your life. Having a passion or hobby not only impacts your mood and satisfies a quiet or creative space, but it also might invoke even more purpose and zest in other areas of your life, even your day job. Winston Churchill is a prime example. As a man consumed with the troubles and toils of a world at war, he was under copious amounts of stress and always had to be 'on.' Whenever called on, Churchill was commanding, self-assured, and confident in his delivery. Excusably hard-pressed for free time, he voraciously stole it where he could. One of his greatest passions was painting; it naturally helped him slow down and think clearly. He often attributed this pastime as having a significant effect on his leadership.

> To be really happy and really safe, one ought to have at least two or three hobbies, and they must all be real. It is no use starting late in life to say: 'I will take an interest in this or that.' Such an attempt only aggravates the strain of mental effort.[2]

> Broadly speaking, human beings may be divided into three classes: those who are toiled to death, those who are worried to death and those who are bored to death.[3]

> Yet to both classes the need of an alternative outlook, of a change of atmosphere, of a diversion of effort, is essential for anyone and everyone.[4]

> Many men have found great advantage in practicing a handicraft for pleasure. Joinery, chemistry, bookbinding, even brick-laying, if one were interested in them and skilful at them, would give a real relief to the overtired brain. But best of all and easiest to procure are sketching and painting in all their forms. I consider myself very lucky I have been able to develop this new taste and pastime.[5]

What Churchill doesn't touch on (and could've benefitted from) is how exercise offers a good counterbalance. It forces you to get out of the house and away from any adverse situations that might easily trigger familiar, crippling responses. Running afforded me the opportunity to avoid situations where I might be alone by myself for long periods of time. It meant I could focus my thoughts elsewhere in a way that would beckon me without being overpowering the way an addiction would. A passion invigorates, while an addiction enervates. Passion can sap an addiction's power, making it easier to overcome. The more time I spent running and training, the more my attention focused elsewhere.

I love what Rick Warren says in his closing chapter in his book *The Purpose Driven Life*:

> Living on purpose is the only way to *really* live. Everything else is just existing. Most people struggle with three basic issues in life. The first is identity: 'Who am I?' The second is importance: 'Do I matter?' The third is impact: 'What is my place in life?'[6]

Naturally, the answers to those questions are proposed by him in the preceding chapters of his book, but offering any kind of silver bullet here isn't my intention. That's a journey for you to explore and one I hope you begin to take. Start by asking yourself those three questions, because when you do you'll realise that life is meant to be enjoyed instead of merely endured. Purpose is a true healer. It has been for me. Ironically, writing this book has helped to heal me. It has given me a purpose, a sense of impact I hope to impart on the world regardless of how many copies are sold. Most of all, it has substituted the void that I used to fill with an unwanted addiction—an addiction that robbed my identity, made me feel worthless and gave me no place in life. Its only purpose was that I would have none.

Purpose

One way you can help your partner or spouse focus on something other than their addiction is by assisting them in discovering a passion or purpose. If they find that they are aimlessly sitting around the house all day or not focussing their attention on things that edify, it might help to encourage them to discover what does. A man without a passion is a man without a purpose. Futility is a dark cave that's hard to climb out from. If there's no purpose in his life and all he ever does is work, he will most certainly look for a release—more times than not, in the wrong place. When he has something to set his mind on other than work, it stretches it in different ways, having a healthy impact. Granted, it's not as simple as telling someone to take up a sport, because even athletes whose livelihoods depend on it have their inner demons to battle. What's important is to do something else in-between the cracks of free time, to cradle a small flame that burns deep inside that will become the fire that will carry you through your career, past the tough and trying times and beyond. Victory over your time is a victory in healing.

16

THE ACT OF LOVING YOURSELF

Forgiveness is the final form of love.

— Reinhold Niebuhr

I don't *Netflix and chill*, however I do enjoy the slow immersion of podcasts. I auto-subscribe to a checkerboard diet to level up my health, wealth, and wisdom, like it's some superpower. With so many choices out there, it's become the new audible blog of the airwaves—a resurgence of the oral tradition of storytelling. Hundreds of topics all vying to be heard. And yet, with all this audible gold it makes me wonder why the world hasn't sorted itself out yet. Why we aren't walking around blissfully doped up on a self-wealth high, congratulating one another in recognition of collective prosperity? But is all this knowledge really making any difference to our lives? Does subscribing to the likes of Godin, Chopra, Rogan, Ferris, Harris, or Oprah make us believe we're any more productive? Or does it give us a false sense of hope when all we're really doing is hopping around from one motivational pod to the next? Of course, it's addictive; getting good vibes straight to our ear makes us feel mentally healthy. But what are we doing with this flurry of information? Are we letting it pass through one ear and out the other, or are we pausing to take responsibility and put what we've learned into practice?

I have made a concerted effort that if I can make the time to listen or read something edifying, I can at least follow through on the advice. One episode I was listening to on my way to work got me thinking enough to try. The loquacious host was interviewing a spirited guest who boomed into the mic about the act of loving herself. Every morning she would wake and greet her reflection in the mirror with an enthusiastic self-flattery ritual. Enwrapping her arms tightly around herself as if to stay warm from a gust of wind, she would repeatedly chant, "I love you (insert your name here), you (insert your name here) are loved." I chuckled in my car as I snailed forward in morning traffic. It sounded so ridiculous, but I had made a promise to myself. I tweaked the rear-view mirror to see my reflection and gave it a go. "I love you, Stephen," I echoed apprehensively. In my periphery I noticed a child staring in the passenger seat of the car next to me. She was fascinated, unlike her mother, who was wearing a look of confusion, as if I had done something offensive to innocent eyes. Of course, I pretended to check my teeth, exaggerating a digging gesture with my nails like I was trying to get something that was lodged in between. I sank back into my seat. And I lost that loving feeling.

The concept of 'loving yourself' has always felt like one of those feel-good aphorisms that ought to be practiced because it sounded reasonable and because well-rounded, tanned people said it. Positive reinforcement helps build confidence, but it's nothing more than belief by repetition. It's not addressing what needs addressing. It's no different from exercising without a healthy diet.

This notion of loving myself popped up again one day as a suggestive prompt while I was having a session with my counsellor. Except her advice didn't require me to chant in front of a mirror.

"What do you mean by 'love yourself?'" I asked.

"Did I say love or forgive?" she replied, drawing the question out slightly.

"I remember you saying love."

"Well, love and forgiveness go together," she said dryly.

"And how does one do that to oneself?" I said, dropping an illeism without sounding pretentious.

"Loving yourself is forgiving yourself. And to love yourself you have to start at the beginning."

"The past," I interrupted.

"Yes, you have to intellectualise it."

"What do you mean?" I kept asking questions like she was on trial, but I knew I needed to learn to get healthy.

"Intellectualising is to crack open your issues instead of trying to stomp on it like a cigarette butt. Figuring out where your wires got crossed, where your views got skewed. This is how you process," she said, her eyebrows raised to see if I understood.

Although I nodded, she gave an example for my benefit anyway. She loved her illustrations. "A detective doesn't hang around a crime scene until the mystery is solved. Finding out what led to the event will lead to the answers. It requires asking the right questions, and that means delving into the past."

Our conversation carried on. I'd ask more questions and she would elaborate until I understood and the hour was up, of course. I knew if I were to get better, to be healthy, to love purely again, I had to start by loving myself. I had to forgive myself. Forgiveness isn't passive; it's an act of love. That's what my psychologist meant by them being connected. They work together in tandem.

To give context without getting too personal,

forgiving myself meant release from all the misunderstandings that had ultimately manifested unwanted behaviour. From all the shame I felt as a child and whatever it was that got my wires crossed. Forgiveness for the supposedly bad things I believed I was doing that was normal teenage boy stuff.

This wasn't an overnight win. I took a while to ruminate. It felt like a contradiction at first, because usually you forgive someone who has transgressed you. Why would anyone forgive themselves for something they were taught to believe? But children believe what they are taught. They see and do. They observe. A child who is abused is taught that they are bad because they are being abused. It's messed up, right? Well, that's a contradiction. But it's only a contradiction until you let go of it. Cognitive dissonance is a powerful thing.

Every one of us first understood the concept of love from those who nurtured us. But it often also can be misrepresented and misinterpreted, over time evolving into what we think the act of it should be. Most of us grew up to believe love is conditional, because we tried to gain acceptance or recognition by doing what our parents approved versus what they disapproved. This sticks like glue into adulthood. And so, when we believe we aren't living up to a mental image of acceptable behaviour, we became unwittingly self-critical and reject any kind of love toward ourselves. History repeats itself.

It's also important to note love is demonstrated by many people who cross paths with us in life, not only our parents. It could be a grandparent, teacher, pastor, friend, or sibling. And one of them might have had the most profound effect on your concept of love.

At a young age, I was made to feel shameful and sinful because I wasn't living up to my parents' standards. Even though their intention wasn't bad, their overprotection and fear twisted the idea of love. The older I grew, the more this feeling would have the opposite effect on my life.

Intellectualising, research, and counselling helped me realise that the more someone demonises something, the more attractive it becomes. It's like the shiny apple on a tree. It's human nature to want it. I believe this is why sexual addiction is particularly prevalent in the religious community. There's so much emphasis on sin and not enough on grace, that this type of dialogue has the reverse effect on most Christian or religious men. It's only now, many years later, that I have come to realise I need to disassemble that mindset. Maybe you need to do the same? But before we can unlearn our unwanted behaviour, we must unlearn our misconceptions of love.

Merely telling yourself that everything is okay won't change anything. You might be wiser and more emotionally mature, but this doesn't mean you've dealt with forgiveness and love. You have to start by truly believing you are forgiven. Forgiven by God because that's his promise to us, and forgiven by you, because God is love and is in you. Then it helps if you can practically imagine you're talking to a young you. It sounds kooky, but I can assure you it's not. In my counselling session, I was asked to write a letter to my younger me. A letter of forgiveness, bestowing grace and mercy. Telling myself that I was okay. The hard part wasn't self-intervention. It was the language I used. It was so easy to go off the rails by telling the younger me things that had become part of my vocabulary. But these words were preconditioned words. For instance, I used the word "filth" in a sentence. Now, although I was speaking positively and with love, using that word to warn the younger me was doing the same thing I had had done to me. This language was taught to me without me even realising it. I was so hardwired that my words were demonising. I was perpetuating my unresolved pain onto myself. I was, in effect, parenting the younger me.

Having an understanding that I was conditioned to gravitate toward negative word associations also helped me realise that I could *uncondition* my response. The same applies to you. Remember, we're all socially preconditioned, so it's normal to venture off, but when you do, bring it back a bit. In my context I hadn't been wronged or abused by anyone. Your situation might be different, so feel free to write your letter of forgiveness to that person, too. Writing to a younger you will help to intellectualise where any wires got crossed. It will also help to bring out all your emotions in a positive way. Most of all, it will shrink the monkey on your back.

I never realised it was possible to love yourself. Nor did it occur to me how to do that. As odd as it sounds, it makes perfect sense. You wouldn't want to tell yourself the opposite? Why would you say you're not loved? That you're worthless? A sinner? That you don't like what you see? Regardless what you think you're still telling yourself something. You're still believing a part about yourself to be true. So why not believe you are loved and forgiven instead? If God's spirit lives within you, then you're capable of giving and receiving love, inwardly or outwardly.

I realised that standing in front of a mirror telling myself I am loved only reflects my action. Watching my lips move as I say the words makes my mind believe it's true. However, my reflection isn't intro-spection. It doesn't show me what's buried deep inside —all the tangled wires that need sorting out. This is an excavation that only I can do through time and with the right kind of knowledge and help. I've come to realise that the more we permit ourselves to take a look inside and to accept who we are and what we find, the more happiness we'll allow ourselves to receive. This is the true act of self-love. It's the starting point to better intellectualise the things that we earlier assumed to be our fault. When we accept our relationship to self that till now seemed unthinkable, we begin to accept the reality that we can change—and that it's not unthinkable to rethink love.

Love and Forgiveness

Harbouring a profoundly negative sense of self hides any authenticity. How can anyone know the real you if your core sense of self is held in contempt? And if any unconditional self-acceptance is painfully disturbed or deficient, you won't be happy with your life which makes it impossible to love yourself. We're all familiar with the adage that you can't love someone else until you love yourself. Opening yourself up is infectious; it prompts others to reciprocate in love. I can't speak for all addictions, but I believe there is a vacancy in accepting oneself, which, in my opinion, is interchangeable with loving oneself. The same goes for love and forgiveness. Whether you've been wronged or are the one who has wronged, you can only heal and move forward when love and forgiveness enter the frame. Loving yourself is about understanding yourself. Understanding your journey of what shaped you. This is part of intellectualising. It takes time to unpack and move forward. Paul speaks of love being patient and rejoicing in truth—rejoicing in the truth that you are not a failure, because, most of all, love never fails.

ACKNOWLEDGMENTS

I'm grateful to my beautiful wife who supported me in telling this story. Your encouragement and overflowing love kept me writing through the days when I was not motivated to carry on. And, not forgetting the countless times you reread my manuscript—every suggestion, tweak, and edit was invaluable.

A huge thank you to my publisher for going over each thought and helping me believe this was a story worth telling. And, not forgetting my editors Andrew and Trinity, thank you for taking the time to read this book; for agreeing, disagreeing and compromising. We got there in the end.

I appreciate all my friends around the world who backed me, the conversations I had, the wisdom shared and the hours spent listening.

Thank you to those who are daring enough to pick up this book, I wrote this not to tell you what to think, but to give you something to think upon. It has changed me for the better and I only wish the same for you.

And lastly to my mother who never stopped believing in my ability to write. You spotted something when I was a young boy and it all started with an essay in English class.

Thank you.

NOTES

Introduction

1. Fight the New Drug, 'Russell Brand Talks Sex, Softcore & Hardcore Porn' [video], YouTube (uploaded 23 February 2015), https://www.youtube.com/watch?v=5kvzamjQW9M.

1. The Subject of Objectivity

1. Andrew Brown, 'Death on the Road, Porn on the Phone: A Perfect Tableau of Modern Loneliness,' *The Guardian*, 8 February 2016, https://www.theguardian.com/commentisfree/2016/feb/08/death-porn-video-phone-loneliness-sex.
2. Brown, 'Death on the Road.'
3. Brown, 'Death on the Road.'

2. The Reality with Fantasy

1. Entertainment Software Association, 'Unparalleled Research on a Growing Community,' 2016 annual report, http://www.theesa.com/wp-content/uploads/2017/09/ESA-AnnualReport-Digital-91917.pdf, 13.
2. Fantasy Sports Trade Association, 'Fantasy Sports Demographic Information,' https://fsta.org/research/industry-demographics/.
3. Size of the online gambling market from 2009 to 2020 (in billion U.S. dollars) https://www.statista.com/statistics/270728/market-volume-of-online-gaming-worldwide/

3. I Never Kissed Dating Goodbye

1. https://joshharris.com/statement/

5. Wandering Eyes

1. Karol Wojtyla, *Love and Responsibility*, trans. HT Willetts (San Francisco: Ignatius Press, 1993), 78-79.
2. The leg-spinner's prize weapon - bowled properly, a googly is almost undetectable. In cricket, a googly, or "wrong'un", is a delivery which looks like a normal leg-spinner but actually turns towards the batsmen, like an off-break, rather than away from the   bat. http://news.bbc.co.uk/sport2/hi/cricket/skills/4173812.stm

7. Welcome to Rat Park

1. David Ellefson and Joel McIver, *My Life with Deth: Discovering Meaning in a Life of Rock & Roll* (New York: Howard Books, 2013), 214.

9. The Art of Distraction

1. 1. C. S. Lewis, *The Screwtape Letters* (London: William Collins), 43.
2. Ibid.

13. Toxicity of Plasticity

1. 1. Judith A. Reisman, 'The Brain Science behind Pornography Addiction and the Effects of Addiction on Families and Communities,' 18 November 2004, http://www.drjudithreisman.com/archives/Senate-Testimony-20041118.pdf.

2. Belinda Luscombe, 'Porn and the Threat to Virility,' *Time Magazine*, 11 April 2016.
3. Ibid., 44.
4. Ibid., 44.
5. Ibid., 45.
6. Ibid., 46.
7. University of Montreal. (2009, December 1). Are the effects of pornography negligible?. *ScienceDaily*. Retrieved from www.-sciencedaily.com/releases/2009/12/091201111202.htm
8. Gary Wilson, 'The Great Porn Experiment' [video], YouTube, (uploaded 16 May 2012), https://www.youtube.com/watch?v=wSF82AwSDiU.
9. Royal Society For Public Health, '#Status of Mind: Social Media and Young People's Mental Health and Wellbeing,' https://www.rsph.org.uk/uploads/assets/uploaded/62be270a-a55f-4719-ad668c2ec7a74c2a.pdf.

14. Does Your Story Repeat Itself?

1. https://www.cancer.org.au/about-cancer/types-of-cancer/skin-cancer.html
2. Jay Stringer, "What Your Sexual Fantasies (Might) Say About You," Covenanteyes.com, September 28, 2017.

15. Might I Propose a Purpose?

1. Haruki Murakami, *What I Talk about When I Talk about Running: A Memoir* (London: Vintage Books, 2009), 98.
2. Winston S. Churchill, *The Statesman as Artist* (London: Bloomsbury, 2018), 96.
3. Ibid., 96-97.
4. Ibid., 97.
5. Ibid., 100.
6. Rick Warren, *The Purpose Driven Life: What on Earth Am I Here For?* (Grand Rapids: Zondervan, 2002), 394.

CPSIA information can be obtained
at www.ICGtesting.com
Printed in the USA
LVHW091837180521
687774LV00014BA/291

9 780648 469209

ABOUT THE AUTHOR

Stephen Peter Anderson is an award-winning creative director, playwright, and author. He understands the power of a good story and that word of mouth is the most powerful platform.

His passion is helping people to navigate, understand and remain balanced in, a world full of damaging distractions, that keep us further from the truth.

He lives in Sydney, Australia with his wife, daughter and hyperactive English Springer Spaniel.

He also keeps a pair of running shoes in the boot of his car just in case he needs to get lost for a while.

For more books and updates:
stephenpeteranderson.com